6/16/07
Jen Cline

6/16/07
Mary

6/16/07
David R Cater

George Reeves and Jean Cline

TWIN SOULS MERGING

A True Story

A Psychological
& Spiritual
Journey

Foreword by Victor Paruta

Cline, Duncan, and Coston

George Reeves & Jean Cline
TWIN SOULS MERGING
A Psychological and Spiritual Journey

By

Jean A. Cline, R.N.
Gary W. Duncan, MS, MA
&
Daryl I. Coston, Editor

www.twinsoulsmerging.com

ISBN 0-9774630-1-X
ISBN-13 978-0-9774630-1-5
Library of Congress Control Number: 2006938736

© Copyright 1996, 2006, 2007 by Cline, Duncan, & Coston
Unless otherwise noted, the photographs in this book are © Copyright Cline, Duncan, & Coston.

All rights reserved. No portion of this book may be reproduced in any form without the express written permission of the publisher. Short passages may be reproduced without permission for periodical, web, and newspaper review only.

Book layout & cover design
by Delaney-Designs
www.delaney-designs.com

Book cover (D) Design-Protected by Delaney-Designs and © Copyright Jillett Publications

George Reeves cover image
COURTESY OF THE ACADEMY OF MOTION PICTURE ARTS AND SCIENCES

Published by Jillett Publications
70 Woodland Hills
South Berwick, Maine, 03908

publications.jillett.com
jillett@jillett.com

Direct inquiries and orders to the above postal or email address or visit our web site.
Jillett Publications and its associated logo is a trademark of Jillett Publications.

Printed in the United States of America

George Reeves and Jean Cline

TWIN SOULS
MERGING

A Psychological & Spiritual Journey

by
Jean A. Cline, RN
Gary W. Duncan, MS, MA
&
Daryl I. Coston, Editor

© 1996, 2006, 2007 Jean A. Cline, Gary W. Duncan, & Daryl I. Coston
Published by Jillett Publications

Table of Contents

Publisher's Notes 9
About the Authors 13
Acknowledgments 21
Foreword 23
Preface 27

PART I: The Story

Introductions 33
The Key 35
The Path 39
The Trust 45
The Dream 51
The Door 57
The Journal 63
The Friend 77

ΤΣΜ

Reflections In Time 97
A Troubled Rite Of Passage 115
Identities And Past Lives 125
The Unveiling Of A Tragedy 139
The Reenactment 167
Realigning Of The Spirits 177
Unexpected Client 189
Discovery Of What We Were 199
Revisiting The Truth And The Lies 215
Experiencing Subtle Truths 225
The Awakening 239

PART II: Scientific Analyses and Spiritual Conclusions

Reevaluating the Twin Soul Concept 255
Understanding Psychic Connections 259
Psychometric Analysis of Jean and George 261
Metaphysical Explanation of Shapeshifting 273
Spiritual Conclusions 277
Epilogue 281

PART III: Appendices, Glossary and References

Appendix A: Jack Larson's Poem 287
Appendix B: Cline-Reeves Life Parallels 289
Appendix C: Super Museum Challenge 293
Glossary 297
Bibliography 301

Publisher's Notes

Excerpts from Jean's Diary have been edited for readability and relevance, but remain substantively unchanged.

A reader may be tripped up by the words "physically" and "psychically," which appear similar in print, especially when reading fast. These words appear often in this text so please make careful note early on. Confusing these terms will significantly change the authors' intended meaning.

The Transcendental Rainbow

In Hindu and Buddhist Tantra, those who have realized, and overcome, the poverty of their ties on Earth are said to have attained the highest meditative state possible—that of the rainbow body.

—Jane Hope

TΣM

About the Author

Gary W. Duncan, MS, MA

Gary W. Duncan, MS, MA
Photo by Kent Murray

Gary began his career in industrial chemistry where he spent five years as a research polymer chemist. Another five years he worked in a variety of settings conducting behavioral and social science research. Following his research career, he spent the next twenty-one years in private practice as a psychotherapist, counselor and sex therapist and was a Licensed Professional Clinical Counselor in the State of Ohio.

For thirty years, Gary has conducted independent research in sexology, consciousness studies, psychic phenomena and western esoteric traditions. He also taught at the University of Cincinnati, Southern Ohio College, The Union Institute, Guilford Technical Community College, Central Piedmont Community College and Duke University. Gary lectured and taught courses on topics that ranged from English, English as a second language, mathematics, psychology, sociology, sexology, sacred and esoteric sexuality, Western and Eastern esoteric traditions, reincarnation, the soul, death and dying, near death experience, parapsychology, transpersonal psychology, dream work, the Gnostic religion and spirituality.

Gary holds an undergraduate degree in Psychology and a Master's Degree in Counseling from the University of Cincinnati. Gary also has a Master's Degree in Corrections from Xavier University, and postgraduate work in Social Psychology from the University of Cincinnati, and an ABD in Counseling from the University of Cincinnati. He has specialized training in chemistry from ICS (International Correspondence School) and USI Chemical. Psychoanalytic psychotherapy training from the Cincinnati Psychoanalytic Institute. Specialized studies in Jungian Analytical Psychology from the University of Cincinnati, Cincinnati Jung Association and the C.G. Jung Institute of Chicago. Sexology and Sex Therapy training from The University of Kentucky College of Medicine, University of Cincinnati Central Psychiatric Clinic and the Masters and Johnson Institute. Gary also has specialized training in transpersonal psychology, imagery and hypnosis from the University of Cincinnati and the American Imagery Institute. He has theological training from the Gnostic Catholic Apostolic Autocephalous Church of North America, North American Seminary. He also holds an honorary doctorate from the College of Neotarian Philosophy in Applied Metaphysical Psychology.

Over the years, Gary has written academic papers and articles for various magazines: *This Week in Texas, The Cincinnati Gay Yellow Pages, The Greater Cincinnati Resource Directory, Journal of Counseling and Human Service Profession,* and *50-Plus Magazine.*

Twin Souls Merging is Gary's first book and he is in the process of writing a novel as well as a thesis on mysticism, which includes his own mystical and spiritual experiences. At present, Gary is an ordained Gnostic minister, a writer, lecturer, spiritual facilitator, consultant, educator, esoteric researcher, and an independent paranormal researcher/investigator. He presently lives in North Carolina.

About the Author

Jean A. Cline, R.N.

Jean A. Cline, R.N.

Jean has been a registered nurse for over thirty years. She has an Associate Degree in Nursing from Elgin Community College in Elgin, Illinois and an Associate Degree in Medical Records from Cincinnati Technical College in Cincinnati, Ohio. She continued to study nursing at Edgecliff College in Cincinnati, Ohio. Jean lives in Amelia, Ohio. Her son, George Matthew, and his wife Lisa live in Northern Kentucky. Her daughter Amy lives in Maryland with her husband Keith, daughter Allison, and son Alex. Jean co-authored several medical studies for the University of Cincinnati and was involved in two independent studies. From 1977 to 1979, she was involved in isotope research for Triangle Research Institute, Duke University; and from 1980 to 1982, she continued her involvement with isotope research for E.L. Sanger, Cincinnati, Ohio. Jean currently works in nursing for a major Cincinnati Hospital.

Twin Souls Merging is her first book.

About The Editor

Daryl I. Coston

Daryl is a sales representative for specialized nutritional and natural health products. He conducts staff trainings and consumer lectures throughout the Carolinas on the use and benefits of Essential Fatty Acids. Before moving south, Daryl operated a business in Ohio, which retailed nutritional supplements and provided natural health consultation. Daryl's work as a natural health consultant helped him recognize that a total person is composed of mind, body, and spirit.

Daryl I. Coston, Editor

Photo by Kent Murray

In 1994, a Dayton, Ohio psychic named Carolyn Shilt told Daryl he would lose his job within nine months. This surprised him, but within six months he was out of work. This prediction lent credibility to Carolyn's psychic abilities and Daryl set up a second appointment.

Carolyn's second reading indicated that within two years a woman from the medical profession would come into Daryl's life with issues around death and dying, and Daryl would be involved in a project that would make him a pioneer in some new area. Daryl asked how he would meet this woman and Carolyn indicated he would meet her in a class he would be teaching.

Almost two years later, Jean A. Cline enrolled in a psychic phenomena course taught by Daryl's life partner, Gary Duncan.

Despite the fact it was his life partner teaching the class and not himself, Daryl nonetheless realized Jean was the woman Carolyn had foretold. Jean was from the medical profession. She was a nurse and had been one for decades. Jean came to Gary with issues surrounding the death of her friend. By agreeing to be the manuscript editor for this book, Daryl became a pioneer in a new area of research, just as Carolyn had predicted.

Daryl holds a B.S. in Psychology from the University of Cincinnati and presently resides in North Carolina.

A Psychological & Spiritual Journey

9/28/06

A TESTIMONIAL by Carolyn Shilt

Daryl Coston was back again for another "reading". The first time was rather basic. A job change and information from the other side. But the second reading was entirely different. Daryl brought his partner, Gary Duncan along for moral support. Gary was a skeptic, which I love because I always want people to think for themselves. He remained in the living room while Daryl and I went into the family room. Information conveyed in that reading was about a life challenging change for both Daryl and his partner, Gary Duncan. They would become pioneers in a new field that up to this time had never even been heard about let alone explored.

As I "tuned in" connecting to the information coming through for Daryl, Daryl was told he and Gary had a mission together. They would need to embrace this with faith and enthusiasm. It would alter their lives and change their perspective regarding the spiritual/physical world they knew. They would met a woman in the medical field who would have a complex situation she did not undertand. I stated Daryl would be teaching a class somewhere and this woman would be in the class. (I was a little off here). I was picking up Gary's energy from him being in the other room. Actually, that part was about him. He was the one who would teach the class. This woman would present a very real challenge where much research would be involved. The subject matter was very sensitive. It would involve a spiritual connection between this woman and someone who had died. The woman's problems would center around issues of death and dying. But not because of a fear she had of dying. It was much more complex. It would be different needing careful exploration and open mindedness. Everything she would say would be found absolutely valid. Factual information would lead them to solving a mystery around death. Daryl and Gary would be pioneers in this new field. A book about this experience was to be written. Later, it would be turned into a movie. Both Gary and Daryl would become very well known.

The woman was clearly shown to me and described to Daryl. She would have dark hair, be rather big-boned, tall and extremely intelligent. She would also be disturbed and confused about her connection with someone from the otherside. Gary would have to really delve into this situation professionally using his tools earned in the field of psychology. Then the information would be shared with the general public. It would safely help people understand that life does exist in another dimension. This would be a great journey for both Gary and Daryl helping them grow and giving them tremendous insights into the spiritual world. It absolutely connects all of us to one another even in death and their research would clarify the missing link between our physical existence and our spiritual selves.

TΣM

Acknowledgments

The authors and publisher would like to acknowledge all those who have contributed to this work, either directly or through their unwavering support. In no particular order, we'd like to thank:

Carolyn Shilt for her psychic prophetic insights, as well as her later consultations on the book project.

Rob Tartz for his continual consultation on the case as well as his insights on the manuscript's structure.

Dr. Stanley Krippner of the Saybrook Institute for his critical review of the original manuscript.

Dr. George Lester who was the outside Clinical Psychologist consulted on the case. Dr. Lester's input was critical in assessing the mental status of both Jean A. Cline and the spirit with whom she is merging.

Jim Hambrick of the Super Museum in Metropolis, Illinois for his help in identifying the spirit connected with Jean. Jim constructed specific questions to test the spirit's knowledge. The spirit, through Jean, was able to answer all of Jim's questions correctly confirming his identity.

Bunny Hall for her contributions and insights into the concept of twin souls.

All those interviewed who claimed to be twin souls.

Dr. Joseph Iuvara for his philosophical insights during the early stages of the project.

Bill Wilson, Neil Jenkinson, Marquita Asher, and Judy Stamper for reviewing the early versions of the manuscript.

Joanne Wilson for her legal expertise.

Bruce A. Moen for his consultation on after death issues.

Rick Spector for donating pictures.

Jim Nolt for advising on the project.

Michael Bifulco for permission to use pictures from his book in ours.

James Powers of the Boyd County Library, Ashland, Kentucky.

Richard Maranville an independent researcher in Galesburg, Illinois.

Stephen Wagner from paranormal.about.com for helping generate support for this project.

Victor Paruta for appearing with us on our TV interview, for having us as his Victory of Light Psychic Festival, and for readily agreeing to write the Foreword to this book.

Jeff D. for his interest and support.

Jeremy from paranormalmagazine.com for his support in helping us get the word out.

Barbara Trush for proofreading the manuscript.

Pamela Trush for her work on the cover design and book layout.

Foreword

Plato, in his discourse on love, wrote of a time when there was a third sex, which was the union of male and female in one body. But Zeus chose to diminish these androgynous beings by splitting them into individual male and female souls.

Plato further explains that when one meets his other half, the pair are "lost in an amazement of love, friendship, and intimacy…yet they cannot explain what they desire of one another. For their mutual yearning does not appear to be the desire of lovers' intercourse, but of something else…"

Edgar Cayce, the Sleeping Prophet, also spoke of twin souls, revealing that Jesus and his mother Mary were, indeed, twin souls. He also said that in the beginning the "male and female were as in one," but eventually became separated into two genders.

We are born with a desire for wholeness—a yearning to unite with something or someone that will complete us. This desire is reflected in the cosmologies and myths of cultures throughout history. It is the search for the Holy Grail. We attempt to find it through love and relationships, and yet these often leave us wanting. This yearning leads many to the spiritual path and, hopefully, a return to wholeness—long since lost in mythic time.

Twin Souls Merging is a journey of self-discovery taken by psychotherapist Gary Duncan and his client, Jean Cline, who came to Gary about her ongoing inner dialogue and intimate relationship with the spirit of a dead man. His presence had existed inside her as an inner voice since his mysterious and infamous death when she was 13 years old.

What is a highly educated and experienced therapist to do when a client makes such an admission? Gary's initial judgment: Jean was delusional and possibly psychotic; George, a fragment of her own personality.

The line between mental illness and mystic experience is at times a very thin one. Both experiences are very personal. To describe one's mystic experience to someone else is to take the risk of being misunderstood, ridiculed or even condemned. But to those who experience them, these are unforgettable peak experiences which forever stretch their concept of reality, their paradigm. Many have had such peak experiences spontaneously, through spiritual practices such as chanting, meditating, praying and through transpersonal approaches such as shamanic journeying, past life regression, and holotropic breath work.

The *American Heritage Dictionary* defines paradigm as, "A set of assumptions, concepts, values, and practices that constitutes a way of viewing reality for the community that shares them, especially in an intellectual discipline." When current paradigms are challenged by anomalies such as the one presented in this book, then they must change in order to explain the problem which the old paradigm can not. This is called a paradigm shift.

Little did Gary Duncan realize in their early sessions, that his experience with Jean Cline and her "friend" would catalyze in him a paradigm shift so profound that he would leave the field of psychotherapy altogether.

Clients often draw their psychotherapists into uncharted territory to reveal a vast realm previously unknown. This happened to psychiatrist Brian Weiss when his clients started to contact their spirit guides and spontaneously regress to past lives during hypnosis sessions. His bestselling book *Many Lives, Many Masters* presented his discovery to the world at large, forever changing the mass consciousness. This also happened to the late John Mack, M.D., Pulitzer Prize-winning author and professor of psychiatry at Harvard Medical School. He became convinced that the alien abduction encounters of his patients actually happened and wrote the books *Abduction* and *Passport to the Cosmos*. Perhaps this book will do the same for the concept of twin souls.

I found my feelings toward Jean and Gary shift dramatically as I read this book. I questioned Jean's sanity and Gary's methodology all the way to the exciting climax of their journey—their visit to the Super Museum in Metropolis, IL where Gary finally sees proof that the spirit of George Reeves is, indeed, real and present.

Reading Jean's diary and Gary's confidential case notes provides the thrill of peeping into a world not meant to be seen. I applaud their courage in opening their personal papers—and, above all, their hearts—to share their very powerful experience with us.

Ultimately, Jean's experience with her twin soul, George Reeves, is as enigmatic as the circumstances around his death. Is this really a case of twin souls merging? The evidence points in that direction. What will you conclude?

—Victor Paruta
Cincinnati, January, 2007

Publisher's Note

Victor Paruta is one of Cincinnati's most trusted clairvoyant mediums. He appears regularly on radio, television, and in print, and was featured on ABC's *The View* with Barbara Walters as an expert on ghosts and hauntings. *Cincinnati Magazine* featured him in their Best of Cincinnati issue. Victor is founder of the Victory of Light Expo, Southern Ohio's largest metaphysical convention. He is on the faculty of Baker Hunt Art & Cultural Center in Covington, KY where he teaches psychic development and directs the metaphysical education program. He has post-graduate training from the Institute of Transpersonal Psychology in Palo Alto, CA.

Victor met Gary Duncan and Daryl Coston in 1998 when they approached him for his psychic impressions about Jean Cline's relationship with George Reeves. Gary, Daryl, and Jean first introduced these experiences to the general public at the Victory of Light Expo in 1998. You can find more information about his expo at:

www.VictoryofLight.com

TEM

Preface

Jean

My grandfather died when I was two and a half years old. I remembered going from room to room looking for him because he died in our house and I had a feeling he was still present.

One night during my eighth year, my father was out of town, leaving me and my baby brother Wayne with my mother and grandmother. My mother had gone shopping after work and then to the YWCA to renew my swimming membership. I remained home, watching television as my grandmother got Wayne ready for bed.

The doorbell rang.

I opened the door and to my surprise stood a police officer with a sad look on his face. As a chill ran up my spine, I had an inner knowing there was something horribly wrong. The police officer gently asked if he could speak with an adult. I turned, trembling, and ran for my grandmother . . .

PART I

The Story

6/16 Things basically went off. B's a bitch. D woke me up @ 2am Holding me tight weepy saying he is sorry to have to put me through this on Loves me so much. Doesn't really want me to see it all. Matt OK Told him he could watch or not as he wanted. D came out right away. Gary didn't need to do anything, just prompted on where he was & what was going on. Spent time on why the fake shooty thing @ all. Started during service time. Went through his anger, frustration & physical process of evening. Surprise @ actual death Actually pulled the trigger @ the same time it happened 37 years ago I saw the house, people D's body after the shot. He really

This story is told from two perspectives: Gary's & Jean's.

Jean is a woman having a paranormal experience.

Gary is the therapist who thoroughly investigated this case, despite his initial skepticism.

TΣM

Introductions

Jean A. Cline

My name is Jean Cline.

Many stories I enjoyed as a child began, "Once upon a time . . ."

Being Scandinavian, I was raised on Hans Christian Andersen and Grimm fairytales. As I continued through life, there was always a fascination for the paranormal. If I knew then what I know now, I would have taken better notes.

What follows is true. I hope that it will give those with similar experiences encouragement, and those who have not yet found their spiritual path, hope.

Gary W. Duncan

My name is Gary Duncan.

Jean came into my life at the point when I was struggling with my career decisions and her experience helped shape my spiritual direction and focus. She came to me with issues around death and dying and wanted my professional assistance in helping her understand these experiences. At the outset, she did not want traditional psychotherapy, but instead wanted to understand an unusual paranormal experience she had been having.

Jean felt there was a presence around her and wanted to understand what it was. She was puzzled by feelings and knowledge she had about this presence, which she was never able to explain.

Jean laid in my lap a spiritual enigma, one I had not dealt with in my career as a therapist. Her experience was so unusual it forced me to reassess my own spiritual philosophy. This reassessment forced me to make drastic alterations in my personal and professional life.

What lies ahead is the journey both Jean and I took to understand her unusual paranormal experience. As the story unfolds, it will become clear it is written from two perspectives, hers and mine. Jean's story is taken directly from her diary chronicling her experiences as they unfold. Her diary presents a concise history of the paranormal experience and how it changed her life. She goes into vivid details laying the groundwork for her current understanding of who she is spiritually.

My perspective is taken from my case notes. I present a record of the various techniques and methods used to explore Jean's unusual experience.

The spiritual implications of this phenomenon are far reaching. However, throughout this discourse, I have focused primarily on gaining a rational understanding of this unusual case. Therefore, scientific enquiry has been at the forefront of my investigation. Only after gaining this rational understanding was I able to turn my attention to the spiritual underpinnings upon which this phenomenon is built.

Now, what lies before you, is the unusual journey Jean and I took together in understanding our own spiritual destinies.

The Key

Seek and ye shall find. Knock and it shall be open to you.
—Luke 11:10

TΣM

Jean

Sitting on the warm beach of the island I love so well, I began reflecting back to the time this experience started to unfold. The key that unlocked the active stage of this experience was a class on parapsychology through the Continuing Education Division of the University of Cincinnati taught by Gary Duncan. Little did I know on that Saturday in September 1995 that my life would never be the same.

There were only four students in the class besides me: three women and one man. We women discovered common bonds of interests and occupation. One of the women had taken several of Mr. Duncan's courses previously and expounded on his knowledge of the subject matter and the amount of information she had gained personally.

Gary Duncan turned out to be a youngish-looking man in his late 40's; not at all, how I had pictured him. He was bright-eyed, enthusiastic and not dampened in spirit by our small class. The class atmosphere at once turned into a relaxed lecture, interspersed with comments, questions and personal experiences and I felt compelled to tell Mr. Duncan of my long-standing feelings about the death of a friend by suicide when I was thirteen years old and the fact I had sensed his death before I'd heard the official news of it. Throughout the class, I kept feeling I wanted to tell Mr. Duncan about this experience.

After class, I waited until all the other students had left and then approached him. He listened patiently to my ramblings and I asked was there a way to contact my friend?

He instructed me about a technique called scrying, which was similar to crystal ball reading. The idea sounded interesting and I tried it when I got home. To my surprise, within a matter of minutes I saw a face, not unlike my own, but male, about sixty years old, and in a Revolutionary War uniform.

It had begun.

The Path

I shall be telling this with a sigh, Somewhere ages and ages hence:
Two roads diverged in a wood, and I
—I took the one less traveled by,
And that has made all the difference.
—Robert Frost

ΤΣΜ

Gary

I've worked as a psychotherapist for over twenty years in Cincinnati, Ohio. Although I began as a traditional therapist, I soon found myself working more in the areas of the "transpersonal," which means transcending or reaching beyond the ego. It was not long before I realized that half of my clientele were actually dealing with spiritual concerns.

It dawned on me in the late 1980's, after a colleague and I started a professional transpersonal study group that my heart wasn't in traditional psychotherapy. Shortly thereafter, I found myself contemplating changing my career, but to what, I did not know. To gain insight into what was becoming an internal career struggle, I decided to go on a spiritual retreat.

During a week's stay at the Abby of Gethsemane, which is nestled in the rolling hills of western Kentucky, I became aware of a memory I had suppressed over the years: throughout my life, at various times, I had contemplated becoming a monk or a priest but felt this profession was not monetarily lucrative.

One day during the retreat, I was sitting on a hillside overlooking a farm adjacent to the monastery. A strong feeling penetrated my psychological armor. The feeling was so overwhelming I took a long hike up to a pinnacle where a large cross overlooked a beautiful green countryside. I stood gazing at the breathtaking beauty and knew intuitively I had a religious and spiritual calling.

My journey back to Cincinnati was reflective to say the least. I pondered how I could move away from my current profession and devote myself to a spiritual and religious life. However, back in the city, I soon found myself in the daily routine with a fixed schedule and seeing clients.

The thought of having a religious and spiritual career would not abate. From the time I awoke in the morning until I fell asleep at night that thought stayed active in the back of my mind. I simply could not shake it.

If I had chosen a religious career as a priest, it definitely would not have been Roman Catholic because I had problems with celibacy and obedience to the papacy. As a youth, I had been baptized and confirmed in the Roman Catholic Church, but later felt the religion was too restrictive. I also felt I needed the freedom to think independently, express myself and have a direct connection with the Divine. Because of this fact, I knew traditional religions in general were fraught with too many rules and regulations and would hinder having a direct unitive experience.

As I mulled over my options, I realized that throughout my life I had studied esoteric religions and spirituality. In my training as a psychotherapist, I had read works on Gnosticism, which is an early form of Christianity that believes in attaining spiritual knowledge through direct connection with the divine. I had felt a deep connection with that ancient religion. The insights I gained in meditation also proved Gnosticism was the religion I needed to pursue.

As part of my esoteric studies, I subscribed to *Gnosis,* a magazine devoted to the study of western inner traditions. I looked in the back of the magazine for a Gnostic seminary and found one in Atlanta, Georgia. I immediately made contact.

I felt I could study for the Gnostic priesthood and finish my doctorate in counseling at the same time. Within a year, I was accepted to the seminary, but shortly thereafter the Bishop died and the school was closed. Disheartened, I turned my attention back to the doctoral dissertation. This proved to be a task my heart was no longer in, but I attempted to continue anyway.

I soon realized I was no longer interested in carrying out the research for my dissertation and simultaneously I was feeling a slow burnout with my psychotherapy practice. I was feeling bored and stuck. Dragging myself to the office was becoming a burden, but I had bills to pay.

Knowing I was slowly burning out as a psychotherapist, I tried to make the best of a bad situation by changing the type of clients I worked with and the type of courses I taught at both the Union Institute and the University of Cincinnati. I was hoping this would spark a renewed interest in my career. At the Union Institute, I had been teaching traditional psychology courses and decided to teach a course on Transpersonal Psychology.

At the University of Cincinnati, I had been teaching a fall course in psychic phenomena, a winter course in dream-work and a special topics course in the spring since the late 1980's. The first course I decided to change was the one on special topics to fit my new spiritual and religious interest. Since I had studied Gnosticism, the Kabbalah, Hermeticism, and other esoteric traditions, I was ready to create a new course reflecting those topics.

Spring 1995 arrived and I was ready to teach my first course on the special topic of Western Inner Traditions. To my surprise, almost thirty students had enrolled. The material was so vast I decided to split the course into two parts. One part focused on various types of meditations and the second focused on connecting with spirit guides and an imagery technique known as pathworking. I was intrigued by how well the students enjoyed the hands on approach.

Based on this course's success, I decided to change my theoretically oriented psychic phenomena course to a more applied approach. The 1995 fall term would end the psychic phenomena course and the following year would begin the new course on the development of psychic skills.

When I entered the classroom to teach the psychic phenomena course for the last time to my surprise only five students had enrolled. This was unusual because normally the enrollment was between fifteen and twenty students. Although this would be the last time I would teach the course, it marked the beginning of a new spiritual adventure because of a student who had enrolled named Jean Cline.

Jean told me about a friend who had died and wondered if there was some technique I could recommend for her to contact him. I told her about an ancient method called scrying.

This is a technique similar to crystal ball reading, except you use a bowl of water and a candle as a light source. You set the candle behind the bowl and tilt the bowl in such a way that the candle flame is not directly reflected in the water. You relax for a few minutes, form a question in your mind, and then stare into the water until an image appears, which can take from thirty minutes to an hour. In actuality, the images are not formed in the water, but are formed in the mind, the same way one perceives crystal ball images.

Jean said she'd try scrying before our next class.

The Trust

Backward, turn backward,
O Time, in your flight,
Make me a child again just for to-night!
—Elizabeth A. Allen

TΣM

Jean

I am sure the excitement over my scrying experience showed when the psychic phenomena class resumed two weeks later. Although excited, I still did not tell Mr. Duncan.

During the class, Gary gave us a relaxation-focusing technique in preparation for some ESP testing. I became very relaxed and, without much encouragement, I moved into a hypnotic trance. My ESP test scores turned out to be the highest in the class.

During break, my classmate Pat brought out a book of prophetic meditations. You ask a question pertaining to a current life situation or problem, then open the book to a random page where the answer is revealed. I opened the book and the topic was trust. That was appropriate because trust was always an attribute I needed to work on. However, to my surprise, when Gary opened the book, he too opened it to "trust." A chill ran up my spine. Did that mean he needed to work on trust as well? Or did it mean I should trust him?

This encouraged me to share some of my experience involving my dead friend. Other class members spoke of their experiences with departed family members as well. At last, I felt I was not alone.

The following week my husband Duncan and I left with my son George Matthew, whom we call Matt, for our fourth visit to St. Simon's Island, Georgia. It was a place where I'd experienced a sense of both peace and excitement, as if returning home. The excitement part came from my long-standing interest in the Civil War. I've always enjoyed reading about that period and especially about that time in Georgia. The old plantations, the churches, and cemeteries were still in evidence and evoked a feeling of belonging. I was always happy to return to the island.

On this occasion, we had more vacation time available, so we decided to take a one-day sight-seeing trip through Savannah. My husband and I had been there once before and since Matt shared my interest in Civil War history, we thought he would also enjoy the trip. After a trolley tour, my son persuaded us to return to a pre-Civil War cemetery we had passed along the way.

I started getting strange feelings upon entering the cemetery gates. A tingly sensation traveled from my head down my entire body accompanied by a flush of heat. I felt I had been there before.

I was drawn to a rather impressive grave site of a Revolutionary War General, Lacklan McIntosh. I wondered: was this the General whose face I had seen in my scrying?

I soon revealed this experience to Gary, after class. He listened with interest and suggested I could be regressed to a past life to gain insight into the pronounced feelings I had at the grave site. Gary gave me his business card and said he could provide professional services if I was interested in pursuing the regression avenue. I pocketed the card and thought perhaps I could be regressed to find out who I was and why my dead friend kept influencing me. I wasn't sure I was ready to find out the answers just yet. My mind was swimming with all this new information. Looking back, I think the time was not right to know the answers.

Gary

It was a rainy December day and would be the last time my Psychic Phenomena class would meet. I felt melancholy, as I walked into the classroom for the last time. The class ended on a good note, however, because four of the students indicated they would be taking my *Dreams: The Night Theater* course the following quarter.

Throughout semester break I would think about my students' various experiences and would wonder how they were doing. One student in particular would come to mind, Jean the nurse, who did the scrying experiment and wanted to be regressed.

Why did she want to experience a past-life regression? What was she trying to find out? Did it have anything to do with the Revolutionary War General?

The Dream

You can't solve a problem on the same level that it was created. You have to rise above it to the next level.
—Albert Einstein

TEM

Jean

The class ended in November on an up beat. Gary would be teaching a class in the winter called *Dreams: The Night Theater.* The course sounded promising! Two of the women and I exchanged phone numbers and vowed to see each other in the winter class. We felt the next class would be as interesting as the first and, after purchasing the required reading materials, I was sure that would be the case. One reason I wanted to take the class was to explore a continuing dream I'd had of a dark haired man. Over the years, I'd wondered if the man in the dream was my dead friend. Would I be brave enough to confront the dream in class? It seemed almost too personal.

Because I was busy with a job change and a holiday work schedule, Gary Duncan and his business card stayed buried in the back of my mind for two months. That would soon change because my friend would soon move rapidly and permanently into the forefront of my life. This, due to a new episode on Robert Stack's *Unsolved Mysteries* TV show. The new episode brought my dead friend's life and death crashing into my awareness. It was about him!

Unsolved Mysteries was a program I saw little of, due to the fact I worked the night shift most Fridays and usually was sleeping when the program aired. That Friday I was off work and—coincidentally—found the information in the TV listings. I watched the program in amazement . . . and with a rather sickening feeling in my stomach. The show did not paint my friend in a very good light, and, moreover, contained purported facts that I knew to be inaccurate.

By the time the class began Saturday, January 10, 1996, my friend had started to enter my dreams. The dreams were very vivid . . . in a way I could not reveal in a classroom atmosphere. During a class break, I revealed to my classmate Pat that I thought I could get some answers to my questions about my friend if I did some meditation. She then gave me a meditation Gary had taught in a previous class. This meditation consisted of building a scenario around going to a house, decorating a special room, and then inviting your spirit guides in. Pat had used this method successfully and hoped it might help me as well.

At home, I tried the technique several times but could not connect with my spirit guides.

During the week, I saw an advertisement for a psychic fair to be held the upcoming weekend. I had visited psychics years before because I wanted to find out why I intuitively knew about my friend's death before being informed about it. I also wanted to know if it was he that I'd felt with me all these years. None had been able to tell me anything about my dead friend, but I realize there are more people in the world that profess psychic ability than actually have it. Perhaps a psychic who is confident enough to do readings at a psychic fair would have the level of ability I'd been seeking.

I mentioned to another classmate, Gloria, I was thinking of going to the psychic fair and asked if she wanted to come along, but she had other plans. I was on my own. The fair was on the way home so I could make a last minute decision.

By the time I was passing by, I knew I had to go. The convention hall was jammed with vendors and spectators. I circled the room just to see what was available. There were all sorts of books, jewelry, candles and stones, much of which I had no clue how to use. On the far wall were tables set up in what was the reading area for the various psychics. It seemed they too were in an era of specialization. Some used cards, some crystals and others nothing at all. There were more than twelve to choose from. I decided to just walk by and see what my feelings revealed. Many were busy with other clients at the time, so I could read their specialty cards uninterrupted.

The card of a woman from Kentucky caught my eye and because she did past-life readings, I thought she might be the one. The feelings were right. Of course, she would be out having lunch, but because the feelings were so strong, I decided to wait. I put my name on her appointment sheet and continued to browse through the concessions.

About ten minutes later, the woman returned. I introduced myself and asked if she could give me any information about the picture in the envelope I offered her. I was careful not to give any information she might use as a lead. She took the envelope and held it for a few seconds, turning it over in her hands and then holding it flat between her palms. She then told me it was a man who had died violently. She indicated she saw a lot of blood.

BINGO! A sudden shiver ran up my spine. She told me this man was present. Asking to take the photo out of the envelope, she continued to look at it and held it between her palms. She said the man was sorry he had not been more help to me when I was young and was repentant for what he had done. I knew what the message was loud and clear. It was the same as I had felt the day he had died. He was still with me.

She then took my hands and said more things about a previous life during the Civil War. But by that time, I was so lost in excitement that I was not paying attention. What I had felt all those years was true! I went home joyful and called my son Matt as soon as I got home. Matt was intrigued by the reading.

Toward the end of the quarter, Matthew decided to sit in on Gary's class joining in the conviviality of our group. I think the other male student was relieved to have another man present. I was a bit surprised to find Matt was interested in the paranormal and I began to reveal more of what was going on in my life. Matt knew of my long-term interest in my dead friend's life, but was unaware of the current developments. It was good to have his interest and support because I would certainly need it later on.

Many students revealed their dream experiences in detail, but I was not remembering most of mine even though I used the techniques Gary had recommended. Still, I felt I was on the brink of something extraordinary.

Gary

When *Dreams: The Night Theater* started in January, I walked into the classroom feeling motivated to help the students explore and understand the symbolic nature of their dreams. I looked around the room to get a sense of the psychological makeup of the class and there sitting in the far left corner was Jean the nurse. I studied the class for a few minutes, reflecting on previous conversations I'd had with the students.

During class, the students discussed their dreams in a group format, which helped them understand the dream symbology. After class, Jean came up and indicated she was still interested in the regression and would be making an appointment later in the quarter.

When the dream course finally ended, Jean still had not set up an appointment. I also found it interesting she had not participated in the class the way she did in the Psychic Phenomena course. There was a deep mystery about her because she appeared to approach me with an eagerness to explore her past-life and then move away as if she was hiding something. There also appeared to be uncertainty in her mannerisms because the expressions on her face and the feelings behind those expressions indicated there was something deep inside she was trying to come to grips with. One minute she was ready to explore whatever it was she was trying to deal with and the next minute she became completely aloof.

The week between quarters was exciting because I was putting together the final materials for the second part of the Western Inner Traditions course, as well as pleasure reading. I had several books lined up to read but one dramatically stood out: a biography of James Dean. At the time, I did not understand why I bought a book on the late actor because I had no interest in him. The biographies I normally read run the gamut from Jung to Einstein, but Dean? That was a surprise.

The week went by quickly. I finished Dean's biography and started teaching the second part of the Western Inner Traditions course. I was excited, because courses on spirituality, religion, and the soul are areas of great interest. That Saturday morning I walked into class taking inventory of the students and as usual attempted to get a sense of the class's personality. Scanning the room, I noticed the class was quite large and to my right was Jean. When I looked at her, I got a strong feeling she was ready to set up the appointment she had been postponing.

The Door

Behold, I have set before thee an open door, which no man can shut.
—Rev: 3:8

TΣM

A Psychological & Spiritual Journey

Jean

In April I took Gary's Western Inner Traditions course. This class was the largest of Gary's I had attended, filling a good-size classroom. Most had already taken the first part of the course and this was to be a continuation. I thought I would have to hustle to keep up, but in what had become usual fashion, it started easily and informally.

During the first class, Gary told us our next class would include a meditation. Maybe the door would open then and my spirit guide would appear?

I eagerly read and prepared for the next class and, when the day came, I felt ready to meet the challenge. Gary gave us the meditation scenario and the relaxation technique. We were allowed twenty minutes to experience the exercise and then he would bring us back to the waking state. He counted us into the meditation and I saw the house I had created in my home meditations—the same house where my spirit guides had yet to appear.

I was walking down a brick walkway toward a large, stone English manor house. The path was abloom with fragrant flowers in reds, pinks and whites. The property was surrounded by old oak trees and a gentle breeze was blowing; just enough to caress my skin and make me want to sit and enjoy the beauty of the day. I climbed the wide flagstone steps to the massive oak double doors. It was carved with grape clusters and vines that swirled over the raised panels.

One door was open revealing a wide entry carpeted in plush forest green and a large crystal chandelier with many hanging prisms reflecting the light. A double curved stairway beckoned me upward past Monet style paintings and various portraits. The walls were divided into a cream color with a burgundy *fleur-de-lis* pattern above the chair rail. The lower portion was a hunter green. At the landing I turned and went down a similarly decorated hall to the last room on the right; a place I had been during all my previous meditations. This door also had a grape and vine motif.

I entered the familiar room with its large oak-mantled fireplace. I saw myself in the gilded oval mirror through the open door behind. The room was decorated in shades of mauve and blue with an oak desk, built-in bookcases and a large four-poster bed. Light streamed in through three large casement windows, which provided a view of the plush expanse of the lawn beyond. I sat on one of the twin mauve moiré love seats that faced each other in front of the fireplace. They were soft and downy. I would have enjoyed relaxing there. However, a knock came to the door.

I said, "Come in!"

The door opened to reveal my spirit guides. I instantly recognized my beloved dead friend as my male guide and a young girl with braided yellow hair in a Swiss-style outfit as my female guide. The girl was someone I had seen in a dream by the name of Marjorie.

My dead friend smiled in his usual disarming fashion and said in a voice I knew so well, "I'm the one you've been looking for."

I stood up, took his hand, and was about to speak. Then Gary's voice drew me back into the classroom.

Gary asked volunteers to reveal their experiences. I raised my hand, lump in my throat, tears in my eyes, and I related my experience. I do not remember much of what happened during the rest of the class. I kept thinking about the barrier I had just broken through and how it was going to change my life. I do recall speaking briefly with Gary after class and he suggested I should start keeping a journal. Since I had already started keeping a journal in the dream class, it was already in motion. The door was open and I was going to walk through it as often as possible. All I needed to do was go back to the room.

Gary

During the first class period, I taught a guided meditation I had used in the previous course, which would enable the students to get in touch with their spirit guides. In the guided meditation, I took the students on an inward journey to a special room in their imagination, where they would be able to contact and communicate with their spirit guides. The guided meditation was designed to put the psyche in a receptive state in order to have the inner experience.

After the meditation, I asked the students if they would volunteer to discuss their experiences. Jean appeared to be in a daze as if she were in a trance.

Jean eventually came back to ordinary consciousness and participated in the class discussions, but still appeared to be in a slightly altered state by the far away look in her eyes. She explained the guided meditation allowed her to experience her friend clearly, which had been impossible before. She was able to have a dialogue with him and he spoke to her in a most clear and concise manner.

The following week, Jean finally called and set up the past life regression appointment. It would be for Wednesday, April 17. An odd thing about the call: I picked up the phone to make an out going call and discovered Jean already on the line. A coincidence?

In the next class meeting, Jean brought her son Matthew and asked would it be okay if he sat in on the course. Since registration was closed and the class was filled, I assured her that would be fine and as it turned out, he contributed much to class discussions.

I lectured on how the Gnostic movement spread from the Middle East into Europe during the renaissance, and presented some rituals the Hermetic Gnostics used to protect them from negative forces. I also explained how these Gnostic protection rituals could be used in conjunction with the guided meditation to keep out unwanted energy influences.

When I first teach guided imagery and meditation, I use a backward count from ten to one to take the students in and out of meditation. This backward count I have found to be very successful in teaching novice inner explorers. I told the class not to become too accustomed to the backward count, because I was going to teach them mindfulness meditation in the next class and, rather than a backward count, I would be using a gong.

The Journal

The longest journey is the journey inward...
—Dag Hammarskjöld

All journal entries in this text belong to Jean and are taken directly from her diary. All of Jean's journal entries are headed simply by a date, or occasionally a date and time. Where Gary's perspective is intertwined with Jean's journal entries, his perspective, as in the previous chapters, is headed by his name.

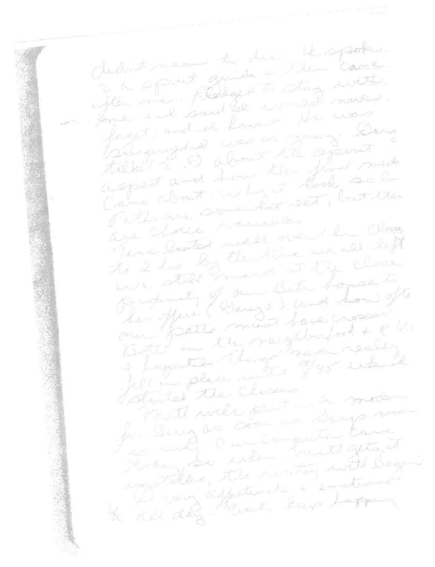

Monday April 1, 1996

Today was the first opportunity I had to try to return to my special room.

I made myself comfortable in my favorite rocking chair in the living room. The blinds were drawn so it was peacefully dim. I closed my eyes and started my own countdown to relax, which would put me in an altered state. Next, I visualized the brick walkway leading to the English manor house and ultimately to the room I had left in class two days earlier. I walked to the window on the left of the fireplace and looked over the magnificent expanse of the emerald green lawn.

Was that a horse stable I saw just beyond the curve of the brick path? I would have to ask my friend. Horses had been my passion since early childhood. What if we could go riding? I pondered the possibilities.

My friend knocked and entered, interrupting my reverie. He was wearing a dark blue suit, which to me seemed reminiscent of Civil War era attire. The pants looked like riding breeches and the coat went down just above his knees. A brilliant white shirt and string tie completed his outfit. He looked about ten years younger than his age at death. He had dark brown hair, blue eyes, and sported a mustache above a dazzling smile. He took me by the hand and led me to the sofa. He said how happy he was that we had finally gotten together, although it had taken longer than he had hoped.

I once heard that to verify an experience was "real" you should ask your spirit guide to do something for you. Therefore, I rather shyly asked to see his movie *Lydia,* a movie I had seen portions of several years earlier.

He threw his head back, laughed, took me in his arms and said, "You always get so excited with new projects. All will come in time."

It was done in such a loving manner I felt if there was anything I needed from now on, all I had to do was ask. I knew winning the lottery was not an option, but I had just won the prize of my lifetime, so who needed it?

Our time was coming to a close. We stood and embraced. I felt the pressure of his embrace on my torso and his arms around me. Then I was back in my living room. I smelled the lingering fragrance of his cologne.

Tuesday April 2, 1996

On my days off or the mornings when I woke up early, I took the opportunity to continue my inner journey. Initially, the sessions lasted from a half hour to an hour. Later, they would increase to as much as two hours and sometimes more. I found myself needing to set an alarm to bring me back to the present.

Today my friend and I sat on the sofa and I began to ask questions. I hadn't seen Marjorie, the other spirit guide in my meditations and wondered about her. He said not to worry she understands our desire to be alone on our initial connections. She will return when you need her.

"Have you been with me all the years since your death and all the times I have thought of you?"

To my great happiness, he replied, "Yes."

He had been with me since his death and had guided my life's choices even to the point of my moving to Cincinnati and taking Gary's classes. Then he made a statement I would remember and use, "Trust your teacher."

I was momentarily speechless. I didn't know if I should pursue personal or spiritual information first. He said it was all right to start wherever I was comfortable. We talked about books, music and horseback riding. I finally wanted to know how I would recognize his presence. He put his hand on my cheek and neck in a caress and I could feel the tingly pressure on my skin. He took my hand and we sat for a while without talking. His eyes were dancing and he was smiling that gentle loving smile I knew so well. Without words, I knew I was loved.

Wednesday April 3, 1996

Today my friend strolled into our room in a bright red riding coat, black trousers, and black riding boots. The pungent smell of leather and horses hung in the air. He embraced me and asked if I could guess what he had been doing.

I bantered back, "You have been riding. I wasn't sure you could do those things here."

He laughed and replied, "You can do anything you want here."

I told him I would love to go riding with him, but due to my current attire, it would have to be another time. I made him promise we would go soon.

We sat quietly for a while. It seemed even in silence he knew what I was thinking. I was wondering what else we could do here? Play the guitar? Go boating? He turned to me and said, "I can do anything I want and I will soon show you."

He confessed he was surprised to find himself in spirit form. I then asked why I had seen him the night he died and was shocked by his reply.

"We've been together before. When I died, my spirit guide showed me where you were. You were aloft in your sleep and I appeared to you in your dreams. I had to learn what was happening to me, just as you will."

It was beginning to make sense. I asked how we should celebrate his upcoming birthday.

"We have many birthdays and many lifetimes to be together. Just remember me and be happy."

We stood and walked arm in arm down the hall, down the stairs and out the front door.

Thursday April 4, 1996

Upon returning to my inner room, I noticed I was still not wearing the appropriate riding clothes. As I walked to the sofa, a book in the bookcase caught my eye. It was something on Plato. Before I could remove it from the shelf, I felt the presence of my friend's hands on my shoulders and a brief kiss on my cheek.

He stood beside me and took my hand. "I know you love to read and someday you'll have time to read all of these books."

I told him I didn't hear him come in.

He grinned and said, "I saw you were intent on looking at the book."

He led me to the sofa and we slipped easily into day-to-day conversation. I told him he was on my mind at work and he said he knew. He indicated I work very hard with the children I care for and was doing very well with the family I was now working with.

I next made a request rather hesitantly. I did not want him to think he was a genie in a bottle, but I did need his help. I was short of work for the next several weeks and sometimes working for an agency brings cancellations. I needed to work full-time and the next few weeks looked rather slim. Gathering courage, I asked if he could help get me additional work and followed with a sheepish statement, "Am I asking a lot from you?"

The response was a wide grin and a look of tremendous affection. "I'm here for you and do not hesitate to ask for whatever you need. What surprises me is, you asked for work and not to win the lottery like most people. That's different!"

"Well, do you help others?" I questioned. "Am I on the list of cases or assignments you have to look over as a spirit guide? Am I taking too much of your time and preventing you from helping others?"

Again, the reply was laughingly positive. He explained, "I have been waiting for you and our time is special and you will never be interfering."

We sat quietly for a moment and a thought arose in my mind. It was a thought I was almost reluctant to reveal and yet could not help myself either. This thought might go beyond what was appropriate.

Gathering courage, I turned to him and said, "You know, I had a fantasy of you that I used for years. In the fantasy, you would come to my home and we would ride horseback through a grassy field, over a knoll, and down the other side to a lovely wooded area. We would continue through the woods to an opening where a small brook coursed through the center. We would dismount and let the horses graze. After a lunch of specially prepared foods and wine, we would spend the afternoon in love. It was a beautiful time and I remembered recreating the scene time after time. I also remembered you had been called a "Casanova" in an article I read and was curious how you would respond."

We sat silently. His eyes danced. I wondered if I had over-stepped my bounds.

The only verbal reply I received was an "Um hum," so I thought it was best to change the subject. Before I could, I was thrust back into my living room. Had I done something wrong?

I was still documenting my experience when the phone rang. It was my agency with work assignments for the next month. It was forty hours plus overtime; my emotions swung between elation and horror. My friend had come through with my request . . . but what about the fantasy?

Monday April 8, 1996

I returned to the room in the English manor house to thank my friend for the wonderful gift of additional work, but upon entering, I noticed a change: an ebony baby grand piano by the bookcase. As I ran my hand over the exquisitely polished surface, I heard him behind me.

"What do you think of the piano?" he inquired.

"I like it very much."

He sat and began to play. "I thought you would," he said. The tune was soft and relaxing, but nothing I recognized. He told me it was something he had picked up in his travels and not from my reality.

As he played, I thanked him for the additional work.

"Things will work out, just give it time," he replied.

The ambience was so peaceful I hesitated to bring up the subject now weighing heavily on my mind. Last week *Unsolved Mysteries* had another segment on my friend's death. I felt it had been a most inaccurate portrayal because it made him appear desperate and out of control. There was no mention of the arranged *accidents* before his death, which was common knowledge. There was no mention of the disturbing phone calls plaguing him day and night, which could not be traced.

I was enraged by the episode and compelled to bring it up. I asked, "I know you pulled the trigger, but who put the bullets in the gun?"

"Eddie's guy," he replied without missing a beat. "There were too many people with keys to the house. There was a lot they got incorrect in the episode but we will not address that now. Soon we will have a long conversation on the topic, but not just yet."

He stopped playing the piano, got up, took my hand, and we walked to the sofa and sat down. He said I looked tired and needed rest. I agreed and had a sense we would not have too much more time together today. Had I opened up a sore spot? Since he didn't appear upset, I just let it go. He leaned over and kissed me gently on the lips and I was back in my living room. This had been one of the shortest meetings so far and again I hoped there was nothing wrong.

Tuesday April 9, 1996

Going back to my inner room was becoming a daily occurrence. To say the least, I was a bit addicted to seeing and talking with my friend. Today I really needed to go back to the room because I was feeling down. Was it about what had happened there yesterday or was it what was happening in my outer life? I really didn't know. I just knew I needed to be with him.

As I entered the room he was at the piano playing *Night,* a song made popular by Jackie Wilson in the 60's. I had made it my theme song regarding my friend years ago. I noticed we were both dressed in black. I pondered the significance of this. I walked over to the piano, leaned on it and rested my chin on my palms.

He acknowledged my dejected spirit, saying, "As the song goes, I was always back at night but now I am always with you. You need to stop and smell the roses. You work too hard. I know I'm responsible for some of that since I got you more work. However, part of the problem is the fact you do it all. Outside job, house, and all the other things included. You need to get more help from Duncan."

Replying sullenly, "I wish I could just stay here. It is so peaceful and lovely. I'll just do what you did, pull the trigger and just get out."

He rose from the piano, strolled around to where I was standing and embraced me. His eyes met mine and he said, "Sweetheart, it wouldn't work that way. Please for me, don't even entertain that silly idea. What happened to me was not planned as a suicide. I did not want to die. Look at all the pain it has caused over the years, to you, to my friends, and to my relatives. I have waited for you too long to allow you to do that and it would be worse if you did it on purpose. I am always here, always! Talk to me about anything, any time."

He continued to hold me and a peaceful feeling began to envelop me. I could sense the bad mood lifting and a feeling of peace and calm taking its place. Then I was back in my living room with a completely changed mood. I was relaxed, smiling and mentally thanked my friend.

Wednesday April 10, 1996

Back to my inner room this time wearing a white shirt, black pants and riding boots. My friend was standing gazing out the window to the left of the fireplace. He was wearing a yellow riding coat, camel colored breeches and black riding boots. Turning toward me, he smiled and said he was going to make a wish come true. He had arranged for us to go riding. We walked arm in arm down the hall, down the stairs and out to the brick path which curved around the house. I had never been out there before. An adventure!

The path led to a magnificent white clapboard stable. Six stalls faced toward a board fence that reminded me of the horse farms I had passed on the way to Lexington, Kentucky. Two young men brought horses for us. My friend acknowledged the men, greeting them warmly. The older of the two men gave me a riding helmet and eased me into the English-styled saddle on a bay mare. My friend mounted easily onto a large buckskin gelding. We checked our stirrups, gathered our reins and with my friend in the lead, we walked our horses out of the paddock and into the grassy meadow beyond. I eased my mount around so we would ride side by side.

"Happy?" he asked.

"Most certainly," I replied as we rode down a gentle slope.

Our horses were well trained. I hardly had to move the reins to keep my mare even with his. There was a slight breeze and the temperature couldn't have been more pleasant. It was perfect! He asked if I felt up to a little canter and suggested going toward the trees, which made a straight row in the distance. I agreed and we urged our horses into a pace, which felt like being on a rocking horse. It made me feel as though I had just been riding only yesterday, not several years ago.

The woods came up quickly. We reined our mounts to a walk and my friend suggested since we had gotten our feet wet why not race to the small pond now visible to our right?

I said, "Great." And on the count of three, we were off. The breeze was straight in our faces and it blew the hair sticking out of my helmet straight back. I was ahead briefly but with the large mount, my friend soon flew by. I nudged my horse to top speed but was only successful in gaining a short distance, when I was left in the dust. We were both laughing as I halted beside him. It was exhilarating.

"Enjoying yourself?" he asked.

"Oh yes," I answered.

He suggested we take the path around the pond, which would lead back to the stables. We rode side-by-side enjoying the breeze, the blue-green of the pond, and the sounds of frogs and crickets.

On reaching the stables, the same men helped us dismount. I thanked my groom and asked his name.

"Frank," he replied with a smile.

I made a mental note to remember his name if we ever ride again. My friend asked if I had a good time. I replied it had been a long time since I'd had such fun and it had been awhile since I had ridden. He replied I did well and would improve with practice. Will we go again, I pondered? The trip back to the room was all too quick and before I could sit on the sofa, I was back in the rocker in my living room. I had the lingering smell of leather and my left shoulder ached a bit. I really had been riding!

Monday April 15, 1996

Work and home situations had kept me from my special room. That wasn't to say it was forgotten by any means! I was more than ready to be back in what I now considered *our* room.

Shortly after entering, my friend motioned toward the sofa. Taking my usual place beside him, we talked briefly about when we would go horseback riding again. I also mentioned an interest in getting a condominium someday in Georgia near the beach, maybe one where Duncan and I had stayed on our trip last autumn. I wondered if my friend could help me with the finances.

He asked whether I'd like Georgia's hot weather. I nodded yes telling him I'm drawn to the ocean. Besides, I felt I had lived there before, possibly in some other lifetime. He indicated I did live there before and would see what he could do to help me return.

We sat in silence awhile. He was very quiet and smiling and I caught myself gazing into his eyes. A sensation of pressure and tingling slowly spread over my arms and neck. He told me to close my eyes and I did, continuing to feel pressure, more like caresses on my face, neck, and torso. I had the sensation of being both there and in my living room simultaneously. It was as if I was hovering somewhere in between, the bodily sensations becoming more intense.

Without hearing it audibly, I heard in my mind, "I love you and I have waited so long for you."

The sensations increased and moved lower, over my abdomen . . . and lower. I became aroused and subsequently experienced the most powerful orgasm of my life.

Instantly I was back in our room, eyes open and somewhat dazed. He was smiling at me and without words he asked if I was happy? Before I could answer, I was hurled back into my living room by the sound of my answering machine. The feelings had been as intense as if a flesh and blood man had made love to me. I felt aglow, exhilarated, absolutely happy, and yet I was confused. It was everything I'd always hoped for in fantasy . . . but this was reality.

I sat thinking for a moment and remembered the business card and Gary Duncan. Rummaging through my wallet, I found the card put there six months earlier. Without even formulating what I was going to tell him, I picked up the phone and dialed the number. I do not remember what I said to Gary that afternoon or if I made any sense. All I really recall is having a feeling I could trust him. I now needed the assistance of someone who understood and could give me guidance. Why Gary Duncan? This would later be revealed to me.

I re-introduced myself, briefly jogging his memory as to who I was and why I wanted to see him. Luckily, a time was open two days later. I now had two days to think over what had happened and to figure out what to say.

Having made the call, I felt I should hold off with more meditations until after seeing Gary on Wednesday. I was scheduled to work the next two nights so, as usual, I laid down after supper for my pre-work nap. I didn't get much rest. Within minutes, I felt as if someone had curled up around my back and put their arms around me. My friend was with me.

I silently called his name and he answered. That began a two-hour conversation about how he had been with me from age thirteen to the present. He told of my life's choices that had been essentially influenced by him, including my choice to live in Cincinnati. This was accentuated by many words of love and endearment. I finally dozed off to sleep and awoke before my alarm sounded. I felt amazingly refreshed considering I had only a short nap—another benefit of my new found love.

I worked through the night without any sense of my friend's presence. In the quiet time between duties, I replayed the events of the last twenty-four hours. I wondered where all this was heading and would it last.

The following morning at home, I prepared for bed. As with day workers, we night people have our own routine. I sleep best in a broken pattern: about four hours till early afternoon and then returning to sleep after supper for three or four more hours. The only time I sleep for eight straight hours is when I'm off work or when I stayed up most of the day. I usually have a light snack and read the morning paper, a magazine, or a current book until I get drowsy, then go to bed.

That morning as I snuggled into my usual pillow-hugging fetal position, I was aware once again of the presence of my friend. There was the now familiar tingling pressure on my arms and back. It moved up my neck and face. Silently, I spoke his name and he replied.

He said, "I hope you had a good night."

"Yes."

He then told me how much he loved and needed me. I was astounded because this man loved and waited for me! The tingling moved up and down my body. At that point, I stretched out completely, still hugging the pillow. He asked if I loved him and I replied, "I love you more than life itself."

Again, I was being physically loved. All the sensations of the previous afternoon were back. It was more intense and this time I was awake and in my own bedroom! I had my *Dream Lover* and the experience was totally satisfying. I felt a peace and contentment that only his love of the previous day equaled. He then let me sleep. As the present began to fade, I felt him curl around me in the same loving manner as before.

Wednesday April 17, 1996

Things were quiet throughout the rest of the evening and work shift. I was barely able to sleep the next morning feeling him curled up next to me. When I inquired about his presence, he responded with light kisses and words of affection. There was no physical activity this time. It was as if he knew I needed time to think things over before seeing Gary.

Then it hit me. He did know! He was in my thoughts! He had known all my thoughts since our first connection many years ago. That was too profound to think of now. I turned my attention to what I would tell Gary later in the day. All this was so foreign and I wanted to express myself accurately. I had read books, seen magazine articles, and watched TV shows about people with similar experiences but I never thought it would happen to me.

At two o'clock I left for Gary's office, a location that was more than just slightly familiar to me. Gary Duncan's office was less than two blocks from a house I had owned for thirteen years. We surely must have crossed paths. I had walked my dogs past his building many times. When my children were small, they loved to go to the donut shop two doors down. Two blocks north of the office was a large strip mall where I often shopped. The mall had many business-related outlets and I wondered whether I'd crossed paths with Gary there as he shopped for office supplies.

The familiar tingling returned. I pulled into the parking lot behind the twin buildings. Gary's office was in the building to the left on the lower level.

In the waiting area, two doors faced me. The one on the right was open and a sign identified it as "The Vitamin Connection." The Vitamin Connection turned out to be a retail and consulting business operated by Daryl Coston, who later turned out to be the manuscript editor for this book. The door to the left was closed and a brass plaque proclaimed, "The Inner Sanctum." I sat on the far right near the open door, copy machine and coffee display. This gave me a direct view of Gary's office door. Although I don't drink coffee, the smell of it was comforting.

I glanced at the reading materials on the table across from me but was too nervous even to pretend to read. I had a curious electric feeling throughout my body. I felt cold. I usually break out in a profuse sweat when nervous, so this was curious to me. After a few minutes, Gary emerged from his office. He smiled, shook my hand, and said he would be with me in a minute.

I mumbled something about being a bit early. Being early is a habit

I picked up as a home health nurse trying to locate a house in the dark of night. I took a quick drink from the bottle of water I had brought along and tried to calm my shaking interior. Why was I so anxious? I had spoken to Gary dozens of times both in and out of class. Maybe the nervous reaction wasn't mine?

Gary returned momentarily and ushered me into a small but well-appointed office. A bookcase, sofa and end tables lined the wall to my left. A wing-backed chair, small footstool, small lamp table, file cabinet, desk and chair lined the right side. Several professional documents and esoteric pictures lined the walls. Eastern music played in the background at a volume so low only listening assured me it was on at all. A human skull gazed eyelessly from the top of a tall bookcase and I remembered the Shakespeare quote, "Alas poor Yorick, I knew him well."

Gary motioned toward the sofa. I almost giggled recalling all the movies I'd seen with the client reclining on the psychiatrist's couch. I chose only to sit on the couch, but still felt I was in a movie and everything was in slow motion.

Gary then settled into the blue wing-backed chair with a yellow legal pad and pen.

After a brief silence, I took a deep breath and got down to the reason for my visit. I told Gary that before discussing an incident that had happened two days earlier, he first needed to know whom he was dealing with. I handed him a photograph and watched as he tried to recognize the face. Gary puzzled at the picture for a few seconds, and then a glimmer of recognition finally crossed his face.

The Friend

Paradise is where I am . . .
—Voltaire

TΣM

Wednesday April 17, 1996, 3:00 p.m.

Gary

Jean was sitting in my counseling chamber. After welcoming her into the counseling office, I took demographic and insurance information, noticed Jean was highly anxious and surmised it was probably her first time as a client in a psychotherapeutic environment. It wasn't long before I discovered her nervousness was not due to the counseling environment but the knowledge she had of her dead friend.

I sat and intensely listened as Jean disclosed with much reluctance and trepidation that her dead friend was the late actor George Reeves. A feeling of confusion surged throughout my awareness as I searched my memory for information regarding this name. I felt by the way she disclosed the information, I was supposed to know who George Reeves was.

Perplexed, I asked, "Who's George Reeves?"

Seeming shocked, Jean Cline proceeded to explain that George Reeves played Superman in the original 1950's TV series. She pulled a photo from her book bag and handed it to me.

After studying the photo for a minute, I began to remember the late actor. I never liked him, but never knew why. I could not stomach the Superman TV series. I handed the picture back after staring at it for a few more minutes and said with much uncertainty and a bit startled, "Oh him! I see."

I made an initial judgment that the woman before me was probably delusional and possibly psychotic. Delusions are false beliefs not grounded in objective or consensus reality and psychosis is a severe form of mental illness.

At the outset, I did not believe George Reeves was Jean's dead friend nor did I believe he was her spirit guide. I assumed he was a fantasy figure and most likely a delusion. I also had a vague sense Jean's personality was somewhat fragmented. A fragmented personality is one with internal chaos in which parts of the psyche are split off into semi-autonomous and autonomous parts leaving the psyche in a disorganized and incoherent state.

As I was taking Jean's personal history the thought crossed my mind that the class discussions she participated in did not hint at any delusional or psychotic features. If she was delusional and psychotic, she had kept it well hidden from her classmates and me. With the scant personal information I had accumulated on Jean I was not sure what I was dealing with.

Jean

George Reeves was the man I grew up with. I loved him as a father, brother, and friend, and now he is my lover. He is the man most Americans identified as Superman during the new television era of the 1950's and who allegedly killed himself in 1959.

I think Gary was a bit startled when I showed him the photo. Maybe he was expecting the face of a former boyfriend or relative, not a well-known performer. It was just for that reason I rarely revealed who my friend was. Who would believe it?

I told Gary about the incident that happened two days earlier, when George and I made love.

He stopped me abruptly after only a few minutes and said, "He's here isn't he?" *

I had already felt the tingling and pressure on my arms. I answered, "Yes," and became relaxed. I felt Gary knew my friend was present, and knew what I felt was real. As George had told me two weeks earlier, I could trust my teacher. Gary next asked if I wanted to continue the relationship with George.

Having thought about it for the last two days, I answered, "Yes."

I had loved this man for most of my life. Now that he had chosen to reveal himself lovingly was more than I had ever hoped. How could I give him up?

Gary suggested that, because of the different energies, I should set parameters for George. George was spirit and I was mortal. I needed time to rest. My time is linear; George has no time boundaries. The only way for me to rest was to let him know. Then Gary rose from his chair and went to his desk, which was a signal the session had ended. The time was up too soon! It was the fastest hour in the week!

Gary consulted his schedule and we agreed to meet the following Monday for our next session. As I was writing his name on the check, I asked Gary what his middle initial stood for. Before he could answer, the name Wayne popped out of my mouth. He turned in his chair with a surprised look on his face and replied, "Yes it is."

---

* See page 128 for Gary's explanation of why he asked this question.

I first wondered how I could have known Gary's middle name, but somewhere deep inside I knew George was cluing Gary in to his presence. I gave Gary the check, shook his hand and left the office.

I walked to my car and sat just staring into space. I had just revealed to a man, whom I had only known on the most casual of terms, the deepest secrets of my heart. I felt no embarrassment. I felt it had been the right thing to do. I drove home with both a sense of peace and expectation. I felt I was on the brink of something exciting and very special.

TΣM

Following the session with Gary, I went home immediately and rested because I was totally exhausted. Afterward, I fixed dinner and was silent throughout the meal. My husband, Duncan, sitting across from me did not ask any questions regarding my appointment with Gary.

After dinner, I laid down again to get some more rest before my evening workday began. It wasn't long before I could feel George's presence curled up against my back. As I turned over, I could feel the pressure of his lips, neck and chest, as he embraced and kissed me lovingly. I told George how Gary said I needed to rest. I hoped he would understand that I was not pushing him away. I didn't want him to leave but just hold me as I rested. George seemed okay with the request and repositioned himself returning to the curve of my back, gently holding me as I dozed off.

Later that evening driving to work my favorite radio station played *Dream Lover* followed by *Let It Be Me*. As it happened, these were two of my favorite songs. Was this just a coincidence or was George sending a message? As I drove up my patient's driveway, I told George we'd talk about the songs after work.

Friday April 19, 1996

George and I talked about the songs. He wanted me to know how deeply he cares and the songs were the best way to send that message. He explained we had a future together and Gary was the key to that future. George said I should tell Gary this in the next session.

I felt more love from George than I had ever experienced from mortal men. I knew that George and I were spiritually connected; that we were twin souls. George explained that since our creation, we have always been together in all lifetimes except in the present one.

George said that in his lifetime as George Reeves, he'd felt something missing in his relationships with women, and he attempted to find that missing something by having relationships with a variety of women. It wasn't until after his death that he realized the missing something was me.

After his death, George realized he could communicate with me by entering my dreams. He used my dream state to provide information about his life so that I'd eventually reach out and discover our spiritual connection.

TΣM

George began talking about a special project he had in mind. The project would free me up career wise providing the means so I would no longer have to work as a nurse. The project would also allow Gary to pursue other interests and have a more stable financial outlook. That comment was very puzzling because I had no idea what type of project would put the two of us together outside of our therapy sessions.

George knew I had been upset with my present nursing position and had been mentally down in general about the quality of my life. He understood how dismal everything appeared and was afraid I might do something fatal. This was very similar to how he felt toward the end of his life so to prevent that from happening, he influenced me to take Gary's class.

As I was adjusting to all this new information, George dropped another bombshell. He revealed that my children, Matthew and Amy, were actually *his* children! My mind reeled and I became confused. Realizing my turmoil, George asked me to bring out pictures of Matthew, Amy, him, and me. I placed the pictures side by side as George requested and my jaw

A Psychological & Spiritual Journey

George Reeves
COURTESY OF THE ACADEMY OF
MOTION PICTURE ARTS AND SCIENCES

Jean Cline

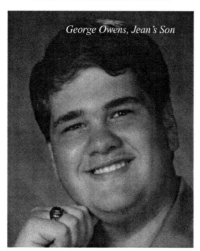

George Owens, Jean's Son

Amy Owens, Jean's Daughter

dropped in amazement. I recognized the unsettling similarities: the eyes, face shape, and mouth.

As I gazed upon these photos, George told me that Matthew and Amy were the children he had wanted in his lifetime as George Reeves, but could not have. It dawned on me that naming my son George Matthew was more than just in honor of the actor George Reeves, but actually the result of his influence.

Sunday April 21, 1996

Matthew had known for some time about my relationship with the spirit George Reeves. I felt comfortable telling him what George had said in reference to his parentage. Matt seemed startled, but open-minded. I showed him the photos side by side and he, too, saw the resemblance.

TΣM

Later, as I was reading the morning newspaper, I felt George looking over my shoulder. I was reading the entertainment section and saw that a well-known comedian would be performing locally in a Broadway play. I knew immediately the disturbing feelings had to be George's and not mine. I asked him what was going on.

In a grumbling voice he said, "I can't stand that son-of-a-bitch."

I asked was he referring to the comedian.

He replied in a disgruntled tone, "Yes."

George explained he had an altercation with the comedian in a restaurant in the mid-fifties and indicated he didn't care for him then and certainly did not care for him now!

I asked George what had happened in the restaurant.

He replied, "I was dining with a party of four when the comedian came over to our table and asked for autographs for his children, who were big fans of Superman."

The comedian had a few too many drinks and was very loud and obnoxious. He asked George condescendingly if he was wearing the Superman costume under his clothes and if so was he going to fly home. George signed the autographs and politely told him to buzz off or he would need a new set of front teeth.

I discovered George had to contend with these types of rude situations repeatedly, but this time it got to him. In this particular situation, I could feel George's likes and dislikes strongly, and knew intuitively that we are becoming closer to each other.

Reflecting on this new closeness, I recalled George mentioning we have always been together and I was to be with him in this lifetime. I wondered what it was like when we were together previously, just before we reincarnated in this lifetime. If Gary regresses me tomorrow, then maybe I would get a clue on what that life was like and what prevented us from being together this time around.

Monday April 22, 1996

On my way home from work I stopped to go shopping and George had me pick up a muffin for Gary. He was very adamant about this. When I gave Gary the muffin, I indicated George insisted on me bringing it. Gary appeared startled but pleased because his blood sugar was low and he needed to eat something. Gary was hypoglycemic and due to his morning schedule, he could not pick up a snack as he usually does.

I took some pictures out of my book bag of George, Matthew, and myself and handed them to Gary. As he looked at the pictures, I pointed out the resemblances between the three of us. After studying the pictures for several minutes, Gary indicated the similarities were very interesting and not just a mere coincidence. He then spoke about the work Ian Stevenson has done on reincarnation birthmarks in which birthmarks from one generation appear on children of the next generation.

Gary and I then made plans for a past-life regression in next Monday's session. I asked if he could regress me to the period just before George and I reincarnated into this lifetime because I wanted to find out the reason our souls had drifted apart.

Later that evening while George and I were discussing the day's events, he revealed what the project was he wanted Gary and me to work on. Gary and I were to write a book and George would orchestrate the entire process. He was not clear about what the content would be, leaving me in a state of wonder.

Gary

During today's session with Jean, George Reeves began talking to me through her. I wondered whether George may in fact be an alter personality, or whether Jean's personality was fragmenting more.

Unable to assess properly the function and scope of this George Reeves identity, Jean stressed her desire for past life regression. She wondered about the identity of the man whose face she saw in the scrying experiment, and she wanted to know if the presence she felt around her since age thirteen was the spirit of George Reeves. If so, was he one of her spirit guides?

Not having all the facts concerning the George Reeves identity, I was reluctant to perform any past-life regressions, fearing Jean's personality could further fragment. Alternatively, past-life regression scenarios could yield critical information on this George Reeves identity and how Jean constructs her subjective reality. With much uncertainty around Jean's mental status, I decided to perform past-life regressions, but only after having the opportunity to gather more data about Jean's personal life.

She was the breadwinner in her family and had been so for several years. In her occupation as an in-home pediatric nurse, she was very competent. Socially, she had only loose associations, as opposed to tight friendships. However, the relationships she did have appeared to be stable. Based on the stability of these variables, I decided with some reluctance to perform the past-life regressions.

Thursday April 25, 1996

After my home care patient was asleep, I spent a quiet period reading *Hollywood's Unsolved Mysteries*. As I was reading a section about George's death, he began telling me he didn't mean to kill himself. He said on that particular night he was having a severe headache resulting from a car accident in which he was almost blinded. He was also in a rush to get things in order because he, Leonore Lemon, and Bob Condon were going to San Diego, for an upcoming fight.

Two neighbors, Bill Bliss and Carol von Ronkel came by that night, wanting to party and this hit George the wrong way because he had to get some sleep before the trip. After an altercation with Leonore his live-in lady friend, he went up stairs to the bedroom and decided to play "The Game," as he used to call it. George stressed again he didn't want to die because his life was finally moving in the right direction after a long lull.

I asked why there was a time lag after the shot before they finally called the police. He explained Leonore first called Art, his publicist because everything was so confused due to all the drinking that night. In addition, they were worried about the bad publicity when his death was finally reported.

Discussing George's death, I got the courage to ask about the breakup between him and Toni Mannix and the ensuing romance with Leonore Lemon. After a short pause, he said things had gotten out of hand with Toni, she became possessive and demanding very much like his mother Helen. George also indicated he and Toni argued constantly and as a result, he ended the relationship. Shortly thereafter, he met Leonore in New York on a P.R. tour and thought she was a hot young babe.

I asked George whether he'd have married Leonore. He said that he probably would have because he was ready to settle down.

There was a long silence and I heard George say to himself as an afterthought, "Mannix that jerk tried to kill me before—well I guess he succeeded this time!"

My mind shut down. I went blank. What could I say after that? I could feel his hurt, his distress, and even his confusion over what had happened to him that night.

Friday April 26, 1996

Lounging at home on my day off, I felt George's presence all around me. He was loving and attentive and wanted to watch a video I had collected of one of his movies filmed in the nineteen-forties, *So Proudly We Hail.* George indicated this was his best performance, emphasizing he was the male lead and the movie had won an academy award. I felt honored he asked me to watch it with him because I had never watched a movie with one of the stars before.

As we watched the video, he'd whisper each line before it was said. I began to feel tingly inside when he demonstrated the romantic scenes with me. He always sensed when I needed special attention. Work had been taxing lately and his romantic interlude was a beautiful rescue.

After watching the video, I wondered if George could make himself known to Matthew as vividly as he makes himself known to me. Even though Matt says he believes me, a personal experience would settle any doubts he may have

Saturday April 27, 1996

I brought Matthew to school with me today.

During class one of the students asked Gary, how do you help spirits that are stuck or lost on the earthly plane move on into the light to higher spiritual dimensions? George bristled at the question and said to me in a disgusted tone, he knew where he was, why he was here and was not lost by any stretch of the imagination. He also explained that all spirits on the earthly plane are not lost like many mortals think.

During the class meditation, George took me on a beautiful vision quest in which I became aware I was flying beside him. As we flew in the spiritual realm, I noticed I was experiencing a panorama of unearthly scenes. We passed over lovely green and pink trees and then a mountain, white-capped with two doves flying over the peak as the scene rapidly changed to a glacier-covered area.

I heard Gary counting us to reality. I knew I had just had a numinous experience. I asked George whether I should mention it to the class.

He said in a rather snide but laughing manner, "To use Gary's term, *process* this experience in your next counseling session."

After class, Matthew and I spoke briefly with Gary regarding an experiment he had tried. Gary tried to contact George psychically, but failed. George indicated that Gary keeps strong protective barriers around him, and it's hard for Gary to let the barriers down because of the paranormal work he has done with spirits over the years. Gary does not want malevolent energies intruding into his psychic space.

Matt said that he, too, had been trying to connect with George but to no avail. Suddenly, Gary noticed Matt had combed his hair straight back—in the fashion George used to wear his hair. Matt said he had not done it on purpose, but it does make him look a bit like George.

Arriving home, I relaxed and meditated out back in the beautiful afternoon sun. As I listened to the cacophony of birds, I began to float and the cacophony abated. I felt George's presence. I was amazed at how quickly this happened because it normally took much longer. I felt very peaceful as George Reeves and I immersed into an experience of oneness, a feeling of connection to the All.

Sunday April 28, 1996

I could feel George's presence close and attentive; he was now able to communicate with me easily. It appeared he wanted to be reassured of my love for him. I felt it odd he should be so insecure about my feelings toward him. Nevertheless, I'm learning perfection isn't obtained immediately upon death, insecurities still remain until they are worked through.

I felt George's presence acutely and very active on days I saw Gary. I think George has a lot to say during session and is not sure it will be said because we do not always know which way the session's path will take us. However, George seemed happy about the way things are progressing and especially how Matt is accepting everything. George is now calling Matt "our son" when we talk about him.

After a relaxing day, I settled down to a comfortable night's sleep and dreamed about George. In the dream, he was playing his guitar and singing. I can't remember the songs but they were romantic and loving. I find it funny I could never remember dreams for the dream class, but now I can remember my dreams and they are occurring more frequently and are more vivid.

Monday April 29, 1996

George let me sleep undisturbed in preparation for today's session with Gary, so I could be alert. I was feeling anxious about what would occur in the past-life regression, but George assured me everything would be fine. Although George helped me to calm down, I could feel he was also anxious.

Before the regression, Gary informed me he needed to know how I met both George Owens and Duncan. I explained how I met each of them and what was happening in my life at the time. Gary then asked how George Reeves had been doing throughout the week. I told him fine, and then Gary shifted the focus to the past-life regression.

Since my anxiety had lessened, I felt the regression would be fun. I had no idea if I would be a good candidate for the hypnosis, but the induction went easily after Gary relaxed me because his voice was like velvet. He used the relaxation technique I was now familiar with from class and then started counting back the years regressing me through time.

At first, I thought the technique was not working because I was not seeing anything, until Gary asked where was I and what year was it. I suddenly realized I was in the year 1840 as a nineteen-year-old girl and was at a party on a plantation in Georgia. I recognized from the scenes that my family had social position, owned land as well as slaves and I emphatically knew my "Papa was good to our people." The scene also revealed our family raised thoroughbred horses and my father was going to Europe soon to get new stock for breeding.

I became aware I was in two places at the same time. This realization was triggered only after Gary asked a question. He wanted to know what I was experiencing and I told him I was at a party. He asked was George with me and I replied he was, but his name was now John. I went on to explain John was the eldest son of a large landowner who lived near our plantation.

I felt I was watching a movie of myself. Gary asked how I was feeling about the experience and I told him I was feeling fine. He then asked me to relax, counted to three and instructed me to move back in time by one day and to describe the experience. I described a scene in which I was having a confrontation with my mother. I was pleading with her to allow me to go to a party. It was a party where I knew John would be present.

Gary asked, "What does John look like?"

I replied, "He looks the way George does now."

I told him John was about 5' 10" with black hair and dark eyes and wore a full mustache. Gary relaxed me again, counted to three, and brought me forward again to the day of the party.

I scanned the crowd to see if I could find John and there he was in the midst of a group of friends talking. I stared at him for a long time and finally caught his eye. I noticed he concluded the conversation quickly, turned from his group of friends and strutted toward me. I knew in my heart as John came closer and closer he only had eyes for me. He walked up, bowed, took my hand and asked me to dance every dance with him.

After dancing several dances, he whispered in my ear that he wanted to go for a walk. I told him I was not allowed because I didn't know where my chaperone was. As we continued to dance, he told me he had gone to school up North and had just recently returned. He indicated that as the first son he would inherit the whole of his father's wealth, which was quite considerable.

I was being caressed in John's arms as we waltzed, then heard Gary's voice breaking the magic spell. Gary counted to three and told me to move forward to my wedding day.

The wedding scene was two years later and I was now wearing a beautiful white lace gown we had purchased in Atlanta. I felt the coolness of the autumn day as a breeze blew gently through the church windows, swaying the skirt of my gown. As I walked in a flowing manner down the aisle, I could see John looking at me breathlessly and could almost hear him gasp.

The scene quickly changed when Gary moved me forward to another year. I felt a profound sadness over the death of our first son. He was born in the summer and John had been very attentive at his birth. His death was sudden resulting from the heat and John and I were grief-stricken. I felt cherished and well taken care of.

Even though we had a large home with servants, I did many of the domestic chores myself. I also taught my servants various skills as well as teaching them how to read which was frowned upon at the time. In return, I had much loyalty from my servants. The house we lived in was similar to the one I had set up in my class meditations, although not quite as elaborate and of course not modern.

The two-hour session was nearing completion when Gary returned me to the present. I said to myself as I was coming out of the regression, "No wonder Georgia has such meaning for me."

TΣM

We were at the end of the session with a few minutes remaining when George came out and began talking to Gary. He told Gary he would continue talking through me because he could not break through Gary's protective barriers and get into his dreams.

George also informed Gary how he feels about me and indicated he had been protecting me from malevolent spirit forces. George indicated he needed Gary's help in this matter because of the vast knowledge Gary has of esoteric rituals. Gary could not understand why George needed his help because as a spirit he should be able to protect me from those negative forces without using rituals.

George quickly replied, "Gary you don't understand what we are dealing with here. There is a deeper connection between the three of us than you realize."

Gary replied, "I don't understand what you are talking about, we are almost out of time and I need more explanation. You are leaving me dangling in mid air."

George further explained that the three of us had a past-life together in the old south. We were friends and had a fun bantering relationship. George said that I would do little things for Gary such as baking special treats because he did not have an immediate living family. George indicated the relationship went sour for a while because of an incident that occurred between him and Gary. Because of this incident, George brought us back together again in this lifetime.

I was tired but had a feeling of awe after the session and spent the night reviewing what had been said. I kept remembering things about our past as memories continued to flood into my awareness. I wondered if this experience was usual after the memory door had been opened after a regression.

I was amazed at the amount of information I received from the regression and wondered what my name was. I do remember a name surfaced that sounded something like Susan or Sally and wondered if that could have been me. To my surprise, I even spoke with a Georgia twang. I also remembered Gary indicating my facial appearance slightly changed when George came out. There was so much happening it was hard to grasp it all but I was already looking forward to the next regression.

Gary

The third class meeting was on the heels of the past-life regressions and I noticed when Jean entered the classroom, she had a far away look in her eyes, almost as if she was in a trance. Her son Matthew was at her side appearing very concerned with what was going on with his mother. I lectured with an uneasy feeling about what could be happening and would glance from time to time in Jean's direction trying to gauge her mental status. The thought crossed my mind that the past-life regressions might have caused further splitting and fragmentation in her personality.

During break, I noticed Jean still appeared to be in a trance-like state by the look in her eyes and the way she walked with waxy movements as she ambled down the hallway. On the way back toward the classroom, she stopped and immediately engaged me in a conversation. She said George was with her and was communicating clearer than ever. I didn't quite know what to make of this comment because George had already been speaking to me through her.

As we settled back into class, Matthew still appeared to be in a mild state of anxiety because Jean was still in an altered state. I nodded to Matthew in a friendly manner to reassure him the situation was under control. I continued to speculate the past-life regressions might have triggered this trance-like state. I also wondered if Jean's guided imageries and meditations at home coupled with the past-life regressions could have contributed to her current mental situation. I was uncertain what was really going on with her.

I shifted my focus away from Jean and taught the class the procedure of mindfulness meditation. I was somewhat leery Jean should participate in the exercise, fearing further fragmentation but kept the concern to myself. Once the class settled into their meditative posture and was ready to go within, I hit the gong to start the meditation and after twenty minutes, I hit the gong to bring the class back to ordinary consciousness.

After the gong sounded, all the students came out of the meditation except Jean. She continued to sit in a trance-like state throughout the remainder of the class. When the class was over and all the students had left, I went over to Jean with Matthew at her side and asked what was she experiencing?

She indicated George had taken her to this beautiful place called Coltran and it was so beautiful she did not want to leave. However, she knew she needed to return to ordinary consciousness, but the gong would not work to bring her back. George told her I needed to count her out of the trance the same way I did when bringing her back from the past-life regressions. Based on that recommendation, I counted

Jean back to ordinary consciousness.

After Jean came out of the trance, we talked about her inner experience. This gave me time to observe her and make sure she was grounded in the here and now. As she related her experience about Coltran, she appeared to be in some sort of ecstatic state. George told her after she dies Coltran would be the place where they would go, so they could work through their karma together.

Once I felt Jean was okay and able to travel, she and Matthew said good-bye and left. I wondered how could this George Reeves alter personality create this place Coltran and where in Jean's psyche did this place exist and what was its function? I began to wonder if Jean was suffering from Dissociative Identity Disorder commonly called Multiple Personality Disorder, and her personality was continuing to fragment.

TΣM

A few days later in session, Jean and I were discussing what had happened to her in Saturday's class. She said she woke up that morning in a daze, felt George's presence and he was communicating with her. Throughout the class, they continued to have an inner dialogue. During the mindfulness mediation, he took her to this place called Coltran and she didn't want to leave because it was so beautiful and peaceful.

She explained when I tried to bring her back to ordinary reality she resisted leaving Coltran, but knew she needed to return to the class. When I used the gong to bring her back, it didn't work because she was now accustomed to being counted out of an altered state experience. George could not bring her out of the trance without my assistance because I was the one who had initiated the counting procedure in the first place.

I was still uneasy about what had happened in class and wondered if Jean was undergoing further fragmentation heading toward a psychotic episode. The thought crossed my mind that this place called Coltran might be a hallucination so I decided to explore this.

Jean explained George told her Coltran was one of the places the soul goes after death to decide if it has accomplished what it set out to achieve on its earthly journey. Since Coltran was such a beautiful and peaceful place, I suspected Jean had created it to escape some traumatic situation. It's common for trauma victims to dissociate and create a safe inner world to which they can escape.

As Jean continued talking about Coltran, it became apparent this place was similar to both Catholic purgatory and the Tibetan Buddhist's Bardo. These two places are where the soul goes after death to work through sins or karmic issues. In previous lectures, I had mentioned these afterlife places many times and wondered if Jean had used aspects of those places to create Coltran.

According to Jean, George indicated some souls remain in Coltran and don't move on into higher spiritual realities because they are at peace there. It was becoming clear Jean really liked Coltran and was looking forward to going there with George after she dies. It was also becoming clear Jean had created this George Reeves alter personality, her past-life relationship with him, and Coltran out of some deep psychological need, probably a severe trauma of some kind.

I was at a loss to explain how all these aspects of Jean's personality fit together and how they functioned. I was certain Jean was delusional and suffering from Dissociative Identity Disorder. I was also concerned she could be moving toward a psychotic episode. I had accumulated an in-depth life history of Jean beginning with her earliest memories and ending with the day she came into my office. Before I could make a sound clinical judgment on her mental status, I decided to review her life history looking for clues that might explain her present mental situation.

Reflections In Time

Like A Child I would listen in silence
To the soft sound of evening as it caught up the day.
Till you were there in the gathering darkness
and we found that our green years had all gone away.
    —Rod McKuen

TΣM

Jean

My grandfather died when I was two and a half years old. I remembered going from room to room looking for him because he died in our house and I had a feeling he was still present.

One night during my eighth year, my father was out of town, leaving me and my baby brother Wayne with my mother and grandmother. My mother had gone shopping after work and then to the YWCA to renew my swimming membership. I remained home, watching television as my grandmother got Wayne ready for bed.

The doorbell rang.

I opened the door and to my surprise stood a police officer with a sad look on his face. As a chill ran up my spine, I had an inner knowing there was something horribly wrong. The police officer gently asked if he could speak with an adult. I turned, trembling, and ran for my grandmother . . .

With a grave expression on her face, my grandmother handed Wayne to me and went to the door. My grandmother later informed me that my mother had collapsed and died at the YWCA. My life would never be the same.

After my mother died, my father abandoned us emotionally. I started using Clark Kent as my surrogate parent. My father continued to withdraw and never recovered from the shock of my mother's premature death. Over the years, my father had several lady friends but continued to remain emotionally detached and never re-married.

More tragedy followed. My grandmother's illness began less than a year after my mother's death with an emergency trip one spring night to the hospital. They had to remove one of her kidneys. Throughout this period, I was often awakened by the urgent voices of my father and grandmother. These voices would signal yet another hospital stay. My paternal grandmother, a stern and detached woman who spoke with a thick Danish accent, would stay with us until my maternal grandmother returned from the hospital.

Caring for and assisting my maternal grandmother with her bulky surgical dressings gave my life some purpose. Though this created an early foundation for a lifelong career of care taking, at the time I had a deep sense my childhood was over.

My mother's mother died in 1957.

Reading became my daytime refuge and the use of my Clark Kent fantasy was a tool for comfort and sleep. I would pour out my fears and concerns to him since no one had the time or inclination to listen to me in real life. This one thing gave me peace of mind and a sense of security in a time where none existed.

My father's mother soon returned from Wisconsin to help out. I had an intense fear of her—like being with a stranger. During her two month stay, I began to realize she was as emotionally absent as my father.

After grandmother returned to Wisconsin, my third cousin Ruth came to stay with us. She was a pleasant middle-aged woman, but a spinster with little knowledge of young grieving children.

Wayne managed to get the affection he needed from the various women who would take over our lives as housekeepers. I was more aloof and did not elicit attention from any of these women. I had all the attention and affection I needed from my imaginary parent, Clark Kent.

In the summer of 1959, my father decided the three of us would spend a week with my great aunt and uncle in Colorado. This was shortly after my father hired Freda, our new live-in housekeeper. My aunt and uncle had a lovely cabin in Big Thompson Canyon near Estes Park, Colorado. We hadn't had a real vacation since my grandmother's death two years earlier. After the usual flurry of preparation, we embarked on a trip I would never forget. It was during this trip that my dead friend first came to me.

Most of the roads we traveled were the two-lane variety, which is now part of the scenic road network. This was well before the current interstate highway system. These highways were identified by abandoned tourist cabins and small family owned motels and restaurants. Travelers today use these beautiful scenic routes to see something besides exit ramps and interchanges. The route we traveled was not always scenic because there were miles and miles of corn and wheat fields, being plowed, planted, or harvested. I distinctly remember how hot it was because there was no air conditioning in the car other than the open windows.

We left on our trip early Sunday morning June 14, 1959. We occupied our time by identifying out of state license plates and seeing who could count the most horses on the side of the road in a ten-mile stretch. Lunch breaks were always a special treat because we got to eat out, which was otherwise rare in my childhood.

Because we were hamburger aficionados, any cafe advertising burgers was a good choice even then. They were cheap and greasy; satisfying everyone's eating requirements. The burgers were served with a big basket of fries and were heaven to the taste. No cholesterol warnings in those days.

The first night out after leaving Elgin, Illinois, we stayed in Iowa. My father found a cabin with separate sleeping areas. He and my brother shared one area and I was alone in the other. I prayed for a nighttime breeze so I would hopefully awaken less sweaty than when I went to bed.

The second night of the trip was the one I have etched forever in my mind. We stayed in a small motel rather than the cabin style my father preferred. It was late in the afternoon and we were in a sparsely populated area of Nebraska. The motel my father chose set back a short distance from the highway. There was a circular driveway that went beside a freestanding office and then around to the sleeping units. The buildings were white with green roofing and green trim.

Each unit had metal chairs out front, which were seen everywhere in those days and now have returned nostalgically. A large tree stood directly in front of the building shading most of the units. To my surprise, our unit had air conditioning, which made everyone happy.

The room was divided into a large room and an alcove. My brother and father took the largest room and I had the alcove with a double bed. The bed seemed very large to me. At home I slept in a small twin bed.

Sometime in the middle of the night, I awoke from what I thought was a vivid dream. In the dream, I saw George Reeves standing by my bed dressed in white with a concerned expression on his face. As he looked into my eyes, he told me he was gone now but would always be with me. I replied I would never forget him and he would always be in my memories as long as I lived.

I awoke startled, puzzled, was hyperventilating. Confused and disoriented, I glanced around. I glimpsed the clock—it was 3:00 a.m. There was a moonlit calendar on the wall facing the bed. It was June 16th. This was 1959.

We spent the next day driving and, though still haunted by my dream, I was excited to learn we were about to reach our destination of Greeley, Colorado. We finally arrived late in the afternoon to a warm and friendly reception. After a delicious chicken dinner and jovial conversation, we bedded down for the night.

After breakfast the next morning, we loaded up my uncle's car and drove to their cozy mountain cabin two hours away. Moving out of the flat lands toward the distant mountains, I began to reflect on my George Reeves dream. I found my thoughts very troubling; I began to find ways to distract myself. One method I used was to focus on the distant mountains, as they got closer and closer and larger and larger.

The next week was spent enjoying the crisp fresh mountain air. A meandering river ran less than twenty feet from the cabin and the winter melt off coming down the slopes created a gushing sound that reverberated off the canyon walls. The comforting smell of pines and the rush of water erased my previous thoughts and the only awareness I had was the pleasure of the moment. Being secluded we entertained ourselves by the busy routine of fishing, hiking and scenic trips. Although there was a radio in the cabin, it was never on and outside information never intruded into our joyful retreat.

After our time in the mountains was over, we headed back to Illinois and I had a gnawing feeling of urgency to get back home. This feeling was about the George Reeves dream, which I could not shake in the silence of the car. The silence was interspersed at times by idle chatter with my brother as my father kept his focus on driving. At times, I was mesmerized by the sameness of the pattern of the landscape, which would trigger a reverie. The reverie allowed me to reflect on the meaning of the dream but I could not understand what was meant by, "I am gone." Thinking about that phrase fed the urgency to get home. The drive seemed endless.

Once home, I ransacked a stack of *Chicago Tribunes* Freda had saved. Then I found it. The blow felt as strong as when my mother died. It was a dull ache in the middle of my being that seemed to spread as I sat reading and rereading the article, which revealed George Reeves had . . . *committed suicide?*

Suicide? Not George! Oh please, not George, I said in silent anguish and confusion. I had the intense feeling I was now truly alone. My last refuge had been savagely taken from me. I gathered up the papers in anguish, fled to my room and cried for hours spending the next day in my room grieving. Yet in the midst of my sorrow, I had a feeling the papers were wrong about what had happened. I was now remembering the dream with greater clarity, which gave me some comfort, but how did I know he was gone? My quest to find the answer to that question had begun.

I was raised Episcopalian and was very close to my parish priest. Surely, he could help me with such an important spiritual issue. I do not remember his exact words but it was explained as something not to be concerned about. He told me my friend was with God and God would take care of him and I should keep praying for his soul. I did just that . . . but was not satisfied with his answer. Something profound had happened to my closest confidant and my spiritual leader could not give me a satisfactory answer!

I was driven to find information regarding George and those connected to him who had been mentioned in the newspaper articles. I spent the rest of the summer in the library on this quest and going to the library was one activity of which my father approved. Being a prolific reader, I scanned every book and encyclopedia on movies and actors. I even read through newspapers from other cities. I searched anything that might have information regarding George's friends and family.

By the end of the summer, I had a list of names and addresses, but for some reason did not write to anyone about what had happened to me. I guess I felt if my own priest did not believe what had happened to me, then why should a stranger. At this point my focus in the Superman fantasy radically changed; I was now concerned with the man George Reeves and not the character he had played. In my fantasy, I now wanted to know how would George want me to live my life? How would he want me to react to my teenage problems? And more important, was it possible for him to love me?

TΣM

In the fall of 1959, I was in the ninth grade; a high school freshman. It was the time to consider vocations and college preparation. I had decided I was going to be a nurse. Options for women in those days were still limited and mine were even more so because of my father: I could be anything I wanted as long as it was a nurse. My mother wanted to be a nurse and my father felt I should want that as well and it so happened I did want to go into nursing. I wondered at times how much of that desire was instilled by my father and how much was my own?

I researched nursing schools at the local library, which led me to inquire about one in Cincinnati. Based on the investigation, the school I chose was the University of Cincinnati's College of Nursing and Health. I liked its four-year program. I was at peace with this choice because George Reeves' body had been temporarily placed in the Robinson family crypt at the nearby Spring Grove Cemetery. I felt I could visit where his spirit would be strong.

The Nursing College at the University of Cincinnati offered a Bachelor of Science in Nursing, which turned out to be less expensive than most three-year schools in the Chicago area. The small voice inside, which had been active for four months now, was telling me the Cincinnati nursing program was where I should go. My goals were set. I knew I had to do my absolute best to be accepted.

My life at this time was occasionally riddled with turbulence. We discovered our housekeeper Freda had a severe drinking problem manifesting in verbal and sometimes physical abusive outbursts. During this period, my father pursued his own interest and seemed oblivious to the troubling circumstances at home. He entertained himself by going out with his girlfriends, going bowling, or attending Teamsters Union activities leaving us to spend time alone. To avoid the turbulence, I spent most of my time after school in my room studying, practicing my viola or going over my accumulating articles on George Reeves.

Being focused on learning, I began to move away from my girlfriends and they too moved away from me as they coupled with their boyfriends. The only boy to show an interest in me sat next to me in the school orchestra.

He graduated before I did. George took the place of dates as we journeyed into our world of fantasy. He was now a combination of Clark Kent, Superman and George Reeves. He took me to places in our fantasy world I was not allowed to go in real life.

In the articles I had collected, I discovered George had made other movies besides Superman and I always sensed when they were on TV. I always hoped the programs would be on when my father was out or asleep. I didn't want him invading my private world because he would sometimes make fun of me for watching Superman at my age.

During the Holiday season of that year, a new avenue of interest opened up for me. I went to a party at a friend's house and someone brought a Ouija board. I had never seen one before. When someone said it worked by spirits moving the planchette over the board to spell out words, I was immediately interested. I wondered whether I could talk to George?

I was too shy to try it that night, so the following Saturday I bought my own Ouija board. I waited until my father had gone out for the evening and brought out the board so Wayne and I could play. Wayne was fascinated with how the planchette moved. We spent the whole evening playing with it but got no results because each would accuse the other of moving the planchette.

We were careful not to play with the Ouija board when our father was home. I had a feeling he'd disapprove, especially if he thought I was trying to communicate with the dead. Freda, our housekeeper, found out about the Ouija board but instead of getting angry, she revealed her own psychic interest. She told us she liked to read tarot cards and had been to a psychic. This mutual interest eased household tension. Freda would read the tarot cards and we would talk about what the cards revealed.

I did not let her know I was trying to contact George Reeves. I was afraid she'd tell my father.

My brother and I played with the board throughout that winter but I was not sure we received any satisfactory responses about George. At times I would even try talking to George before going to sleep, hoping he would come into my dreams, but to no avail. We eventually stopped playing with the board. I felt my eight-year-old brother was too young to help me use it effectively. I needed to find some other way to communicate with George.

TΣM

At the first anniversary of George's death, I did the only commemorative thing I could do and that was to remember and pray. I stayed up until the hour of his death just remembering where I had been the previous year and reviewing accounts of what had happened to him. It was then I got the insatiable urge to go to Spring Grove Cemetery in Cincinnati, where George's body was still being held. Since I had planted the seed deep in my father's mind about going to the University of Cincinnati, it wasn't too hard to get him to agree to take a short trip to see the school and talk with the admission officials. After gathering university information and road maps from the local motor club, we were ready to leave.

The expressway at the time was still under construction between Chicago and Cincinnati so we traveled State Route 52 through rural Indiana. We went through Indianapolis and finally entered the suburbs of Cincinnati. The excitement seemed to build as the miles ticked away. It peaked when the Cincinnati skyline came into view. Even though I grew up near Chicago, there was an intense feeling of coming home when we crossed the Harrison viaduct and turned onto Central Parkway. I knew intuitively I had to be there!

The school interview was hopeful and I loved Clifton Campus. Through careful manipulation, I got my father to drive down Clifton Avenue to Spring Grove Cemetery. I had mixed feelings of joy and sadness upon approaching the cemetery gates. I knew I was close to George's spirit. It was the first time I was able to feel the tingling sensations which assured me I was right. At that moment, I knew my destiny was in Cincinnati for better or for worse.

In the fall, I started my sophomore year as an official high school student. This began a period of great change, both at home and in my school life. Freda had been fired and I was now the chief domestic. It gave me more household chores but with no one at home during the day, there wasn't much mess to clean up. Like most working women today, I did most of the cleaning on the weekends. Evenings I fixed supper, supervised my brother, cleaned up the kitchen and then hit the books. Since Freda was no longer with us, the atmosphere in the home had become quiet and peaceful. The extra chores were a small price to pay for this new, relaxed atmosphere. With more calmness in our home, Wayne also seemed much happier.

During this time, my father began dating a new lady friend named Hazel who felt we should be included in family activities. She had never been married and spent much of her time working in a hardware store and caring for her elderly invalid mother. She seemed to respect what I was doing at home and would give gentle advice when I sought it. I welcomed her advice on clothes and after losing a great deal of weight, I started to work on my wardrobe.

Overall, I had a better feeling about myself. It must have showed as I gained the interest of a boy in our church youth group. He was a junior at a private academy in town and had a rather lonely quality about him. He liked books and music and we had lots of good conversation. He was the focus of my romantic interest for the next two years. Since neither of us were allowed to go out at night, we spent our time together before church and at Sunday youth group activities. This was the extent of our dating experience. He was someone to talk with and that helped me to gain a sense of self-confidence. My grades were doing well so my plans for college were clearly on track.

Although there were many new activities in my life, George Reeves was still with me in fantasy. I had a mile and a half walk home from school each day and since I was usually alone, I started a fantasy with George to make the trip go faster. In the fantasy, I became an actress and George was my mentor. He would help me create roles in our imaginary world, which also helped with school problems and my family situation at home. This role-playing activity with George allowed him to create situations that would give me answers to my problems. Always the answers I needed came through George, either as I was walking home in our fantasy plays or at night in dreams. I would often awaken with new insight about a particular problem and a feeling that the problem would be taken care of.

One of the issues George helped me resolve was my aching concern over the money I needed to attend the University of Cincinnati. In the fantasy I was having with George, I brought up this concern. He smiled, touched me gently on the shoulder and told me he knew the situation would work in my favor. As it turned out that summer of my sophomore year, my paternal grandmother sold her home and went to live with my Uncle on his farm in rural Wisconsin. After selling the property, she divided a portion of the money and spread it out among her grandchildren. Each grandchild received a lump sum, which was enough for me to attend nursing school.

TΣM

The second anniversary of George's death was spent in the same way as the first, through prayer and contemplation. That year the only response I received from George was the feeling I was on track with my life. That was enough.

Later that summer we took another trip to Colorado to visit my aunt and uncle. During the trip, my mind reflected back to the experience I had with George in the motel the night he died in 1959. However, far from being in a somber mood, I felt uplifted and joyful because of the inner dramas I was playing with George as my mentor. On this trip, there was a major difference because Hazel went along, which added to the experience. She made the trip more enjoyable with much laughter and pleasant conversation. We had the best time learning to play Pinochle one rainy day in a motel. Playing Pinochle became a Saturday night event. The four of us would play several hours before Wayne and I went to bed.

Looking back, it seems like the summer trip was a trial run to see if a permanent situation between my father and Hazel might be possible. That was never to be because Hazel was diagnosed with cancer that autumn and died the following spring. This event forever erased the possibility of a normal family life for us. After Hazel's death, my father resumed his activities out of the home. I knew he was grieving for her but again he had no clue as to how to help us. I went to George to help heal my grief over her death. By now, this fantasy seemed to be the only stable part of my unstable life. In the fantasy, I returned to the focus of my goal to push forward and get to Cincinnati.

During my junior year, I applied to the University of Cincinnati, took the entrance examinations and visited a couple of nursing schools in the Elgin, Illinois area. The visits were all half-hearted since I knew there was only one place for me to go. My grades continued to be above average and my only diversion away from schoolwork was my church friends. There was nothing to do except keep that goal in focus.

My senior year was a mixed blessing. My father had a new girlfriend once again. However, it was too soon for me to have a relationship with anyone at that time. His new lady friend, Betty, and I were like oil and water, I did not like her personality at all. She was much younger than my father and a party-type. They were gone most weekends and after a few perfunctory invitations, Wayne and I were left alone once again. My church boyfriend had graduated the previous spring so George once again was my primary emotional outlet. By late fall 1962, I received the news I was waiting for! I was accepted for admission to the College of Nursing at the University of Cincinnati for autumn 1963. If nothing else went right in the next nine months, at least I had my dream fulfilled because I would finally be close to George!

ΤΣΜ

My focus the summer of 1963 was going to Cincinnati and every day I was planning for the upcoming year. Since my only jobs that summer were housekeeping and taking care of my brother, I had plenty of time to daydream about what collegiate life would bring. I listed and re-listed various essentials I would take and for several weeks had piles of clothes, suitcases, and books lining the free spaces of my room. When fall arrived, I was ready.

The academic year started late on the Cincinnati campus. It was also the first year of the new quarter system so there were many changes in the academic calendar. Freshmen had to arrive a week earlier for orientation. So, with the car loaded, we drove back to Cincinnati the last week of September. I was very excited because I was going where I knew I needed to be.

The nurses were housed in dormitories on the grounds of General Hospital. Room and board was still supplied by the Hospital for services rendered by the students. My class would be the last one to get that benefit. The main campus was about a mile away where most of the academic classes were held. No bus or shuttle services were provided, so you had to either find a ride with someone who had a car or walk. I was lucky in getting a morning ride to my classes, but in the afternoon I had to walk.

With my hectic schedule, it was difficult to eat at the dorm cafeteria. I quickly became a vending machine junky. The few restaurants then available in the university area were either packed with people or beyond my budget. A couple of us found a basement lounge in one of the university buildings, which had little use during the noon hour. We would use the lounge for study and would sometimes sleep for a few minutes before our afternoon classes.

We had twenty-one credit hours the first quarter and by the luck of the draw, I was in the group that had classes from 8 a.m. to 4 p.m. most days. Because I had a class on campus after the nursing course at the dorm, I had to make the round trip back to the main campus twice every Monday, Wednesday, and Friday. I was tired all the time.

I learned to take a short catnap after the evening meal, but with studying until midnight and getting up at 6 a.m., I was always looking for a minute to shut my eyes. The only recreation I allowed myself was the Episcopal Church campus group and church on Sunday. I figured I needed to meet a few people who were not nurses to keep my spiritual life intact.

From the time of George's death the number sixteen, which was the date of his death, grew more meaningful for me. My room number in the dorm was 316, but this time it was not to be a good omen because my roommate and I did not get along. She was constantly busy, liked to have the radio on and had lots of visitors in and out continuously. I had to escape to the quiet of the downstairs library in order to concentrate on my studies.

I had never shared a room before and our dorm room had been converted from a single to a double occupancy. Personal space was limited at best in those small quarters. The Waterloo in our relationship came when my roommate invited a friend from her hometown to stay the weekend. She neglected to tell me, so I had to stay in the floor lounge down the hall and soon thereafter, we parted company.

My second roommate was more like me in habits and attitudes and as a result, we became very close. Even though the rooming situation was better and I settled into a comfortable routine, there was still an ominous feeling that persisted.

In spite of all the collegiate turmoil, I had not forgotten George Reeves. One beautiful fall weekend I had some free time so I put on my walking shoes and headed to Spring Grove Cemetery. It was soothing to think George's spirit was there, and just that thought got me through some of the rough times to come.

I immediately began to have an external struggle. The situation with my former roommate, the hectic class schedule, and the long walks to campus were one thing, but then I ran across the problem of college professors. I was having trouble with the Freshman English course. A graduate student taught my section and thought it was beneath him to teach freshmen and he even told us so. He'd constantly look through the window onto the street as he paced back and forth. The only time he made eye contact with the class was to criticize us. In my naivete, I did not realize I could transfer out of his section, nor did my academic advisor suggest it. I thought, like in high school, you had to stay were you were put.

The ten-week quarter was finally over so I packed up, said my good-byes and went home for the Holidays. In my deepest hopes, I prayed that my grades in other subjects would offset the poor showing I had in English. Some of my grades hinged on a final exam, so I was in the dark about what to expect throughout the holidays.

I finally received my Christmas present from the University and it was not a pretty one. For the first time in my life, I was on academic probation and was crushed. My brother and I were alone for much of the holidays but I did get the chance to be with several of my close friends. That seemed to buoy my resolve and I returned to campus after the hiatus, rested and renewed. I had an intuition that I belonged in Cincinnati and I was not going to give up.

Winter and spring quarters were just as dismal as the autumn one had been. In addition to school pressures, my brother started phoning about home problems. Our father had started staying away weekends with his girlfriend, Betty, and was dipping into Wayne's savings. I could do little but comfort Wayne and advise him to call either our priest or our great uncle for advice.

Wayne's situation at home did nothing to help my concentration, contributing to a pre-ulcer condition, resulting in pain most of my waking hours. I nearly collapsed upon learning my grades during academic probation were not high enough to allow me to stay in the nursing program. I was devastated. I sat on the dormitory steps and cried. My heart was broken. I was now to be wrenched from the place I most wanted to be. I vowed to return but had no idea of how or when.

TΣM

I spent the summer of nineteen sixty-four working in the hospital two blocks from my home as a dietary aide. It was my first paying job other than baby-sitting. Working with others in a medical setting, even though it was not in patient care, was a wealth of experience.

There were treasures beyond the job itself. One of the women I worked with went to a psychic regularly and kept us amused with her adventures. I wondered if this psychic could answer my questions about George. Why had I intuitively known about his death? Was he the presence I'd felt with me since that night? The fifth anniversary of his death had just passed and I had been thinking about him.

I got the psychic's address, enlisted the cooperation of a friend with a car, and took a trip to a small town north of where I lived. The psychic was a man. He conducted readings with ordinary playing cards. He gave me no information about George.

In the autumn of 1964, on the recommendation of my priest, I enrolled in a small nursing school associated with the University of Wisconsin in Racine. My priest felt my best bet with school would be like falling off a horse: you get right back on. With his help, I headed north but did not have the enthusiasm I had when going to Cincinnati. Nonetheless I was moving forward.

The freshman dorm was located a block from Lake Michigan. The foghorns and warning bells seemed as if they were in our room. It added to the eerie ambiance of the two-story building, which looked as if it had been taken from a B-grade Halloween movie. The dorm mother even fit the picture resembling Elsa Lanchester in a fright wig. At times, I wondered if I had just dropped into the *Twilight Zone*.

My feelings about my new place of learning were not positive. Most of the girls lived close by and went home most weekends leaving only three of us to tough it out. My roommate had difficulty adjusting being away from home and left after the first month. That left two of us to rattle around the spooky building on weekends. As if that wasn't enough, history was repeating itself, my brother continued to call in distress about being left alone or with some other problem. After the first semester, I was again having trouble academically and at one point, wasn't sure if I could pass any course, no matter how easy.

One weekend in March 1965, I called my father to come and take me home. At 19 years old, I felt on the verge of a nervous breakdown. I could not concentrate, sleep, or eat. My stomach was in knots. I didn't know if I wanted to be a nurse or if I could succeed at anything. I had no idea what to do with my life. I suddenly knew what George Reeves must have felt like in his last days. I felt hopeless.

I was close to ending it all. I wasn't accustomed to academic failure and had experienced the worst two academic years of my life. Back home, I stayed in my room for two weeks just wallowing over my situation.

I began reading the scrapbook I had accumulated on George Reeves and, after two weeks, the depressive cloud mysteriously lifted.

I resolved to find out once and for all whether I could become a nurse. Since I had no car, the logical thing to do was go back to the hospital, which was two blocks away and get a job. Within a couple of weeks I was in nurse's aide training and, two weeks after that, I started a lifelong career on the night shift. I turned out to be a natural night owl and was lucky to be assigned to a medical unit with supportive professionals.

With the help of these professional women, I discovered I loved the excitement of the medical world. It was before the advent of the ICU when even nurses in training were exposed to critical care patients. I was actually doing something important for the first time and I blossomed with the aid of those I was lucky enough to work with. The personal mentoring I received from the nurses in the first year as an aide gave me the confidence to take a microbiology course at the local community college in the autumn of 1965.

The nurses I worked with encouraged me to give school another try based on their observations concerning my work performance. I loved what I was doing and wanted to do more, which meant sticking my neck out again academically. I passed the microbiology course with a high B and for the first time in quite awhile, felt the glow of success.

Having purchased a car in the summer of 1965, I started visiting local psychics recommended by co-workers. The dreams and feelings about George continued, but still the psychics could not give answers to the questions I asked about his death.

During my quest for information, I was inundated with subtle thoughts and feelings about George. For instance, I knew when his movies would be aired on television before they were listed in any guide. Newspaper and magazine articles about George literally fell into my lap, as if someone dropped them there and flipped them open to the right page. Who or *what* was trying to get my attention? I kept all this information hoping I'd someday have an answer.

After my success with the microbiology course, I was ready to start school again. A two-year nursing program had opened up at the local community college. I worried that I wouldn't have the chance to continue on my career path if I enrolled in the two-year program. However, with the advice of my coworkers, I applied for the two-year nursing program and was accepted in the autumn of 1966.

Two years later in May of 1968, I graduated with a B average. I continued to work for the next six months at the hospital in Elgin and then went on to pass my nursing licensure exam.

After the licensure notification, I kept my vow and returned to Cincinnati. However, this time I returned as a professional and not as a student. I went back to General Hospital where I had been dismissed four years earlier and was given the job of staff nurse on the night shift on the B and C Pavilions. I was home again!

A Troubled Rite Of Passage

I'm going home to see if there is really such a place as home.
—Rod McKuen

TΣM

Jean

My first apartment in Cincinnati was less than a mile from Spring Grove Cemetery where George Reeves remains had been kept for awhile after his death. The cemetery was located near Proctor and Gamble and a large housing project. Even with domestic and financial downsizing, I was happy to be back. When the holidays arrived, I went home to Elgin, Illinois for a family visit. Upon my return to Cincinnati, I discovered my apartment had been burglarized. This incident put me in contact with neighbors who in turn introduced me to the man whom would be my first husband. His name was George Owens—another George in my life.

George Owens was a large man standing six foot five, recently graduated from the local engineering school and employed as a paper making engineer for Proctor and Gamble. Our matchmaking friends felt we would be right for each other and after a two-year courtship we were engaged and finally married April 24, 1971.

By August 1971, I had to say goodbye again to my beloved home. Proctor and Gamble sent us to rural Pennsylvania. We purchased an old farm, which included a one-half story white-pillared farmhouse with ten acres of rolling rocky terrain. It was similar to my grandparents' farm in Wisconsin, where, as a child, I enjoyed playing in the barns and running through the fields. Maybe this move would not be so bad after all.

Being city bred made it difficult to adjust to the quiet rural nights, but soon the crickets and peepers lulled me into a delicious, peaceful sleep. Work opportunities there were scarce so I took a part-time job in the small community hospital about twenty miles away. By the time the first winter snows arrived in early November, I was ready to retire and become a full-time housewife.

After our first wedding anniversary, I discovered I was pregnant. With poor weather and limited pay, I settled into sewing, baking bread, and other domestic chores. The George Reeves dreams began to reoccur. Although I was not sick from the pregnancy, I did have problems sleeping. I would read, fall asleep, dream of a man in white, then awaken.

At six months, I began having recurring dreams about the baby. The medical group that was caring for me had three physicians on staff. In the dreams, one of the physicians, Landis, delivered a baby. The baby was always a boy and because of that, we did not consider a girl's name.

On January 14, 1973, Dr. Landis delivered a baby boy. January was George Reeves' birth month and we named our baby George Matthew Owens. Of course, "George" was his father's name, but I secretly named him after George Reeves because of the continuing feelings I had for the late actor. Matthew became the center of our lives as the first child often does. He was a happy and healthy baby. My days were filled with the joy of caring for him and watching him grow. I think my life was at its best then.

In the spring of 1974, George and I decided we would try to have a second child. I was closing in on being thirty and did not want to extend my childbearing years beyond that point. I had a second cousin who had birth defects after being born to a mother in her thirty's. I did not want to tempt fate. I was also eager to have my children close together because my brother and I were five years apart and I was more his mother than his sister.

In July of that year, I started having stomach pains again similar to the pre-ulcer pains of my school days. Initially my physician did not think I was pregnant so he put me on ulcer medication. When the medication proved ineffective after two weeks, I was retested and found to be two months pregnant. It was a mixed blessing because I wanted a second child, but knew that taking ulcer medication could possibly damage the baby. The stomach pains and the nausea of the pregnancy lasted long into fall.

About the time I was feeling better, we found out we would be moving again, this time to Northern Alberta, Canada. The move occurred in January 1975, one month before the due date of my second child. I was not surprised by the need to move because my dreams clued me in. Unlike the dreams of my previous pregnancy, I could not see the physician's face, so I surmised the physician must be one I hadn't yet met. I would meet that physician in Canada as it turned out.

My dreams once again showed my baby being born and this time it was a girl. My husband rejected the idea it would be a girl because in his family most births were boys. My dreams continued to indicate we would have a girl, but no amount of coercion would get my husband to help me pick out a girl's name.

Amy Ann was born in Alberta, Canada on February 19, 1975. It took two days to decide on a name and a long time for my husband to get over the fact I told him so. Amy was born healthy, despite the unnecessary ulcer medication.

The long dark winter days and being away from home eventually got to me. I began to have thoughts of taking the children and returning to Cincinnati. By fall, my prayers were answered. George was transferred back to Cincinnati. By November, I was home again.

George Reeves once again became prominent in my mind, but this time something else was happening. I started having intense vivid dreams. This was different because throughout my life, I could not remember dreams vividly. However, this time I was dreaming about a tall dark-haired man. When I would awaken, I had the feeling the dark haired man was George Reeves and wondered what the dreams meant.

During that winter I started to frequent a local bookstore. This was a special delight since I had been unable to frequent bookstores in rural Pennsylvania or Canada. Springtime was approaching when I found a treasure in the bookstore, which was a new paperback book, *The History of Superman* by Gary Grossman. The book contained dozens of pictures and loads of information about George Reeves and his career, which validated most of what I already knew. I devoured the information like one having a meal after a fast.

As the June memorial date of George's death was fast approaching, I was on my special quest again. I had been loyal to his memory all the previous years, so this time I decided to send a spray of flowers to his burial site. I found the name of the funeral director in Los Angeles who had originally prepared George's body and gave him a call. The funeral director was not much help because the only information he had was that George's remains had been sent to Cincinnati—information I already knew.

I began a quest to find other contacts that may have the information I needed. The only other avenues I found were his mother and a friend named Natividad Vacio. I soon found out George's mother was deceased but found Natividad's address in the Los Angeles phone directory and wrote him a letter. To my surprise, he replied a few weeks later. In the letter, he indicated George had been cremated and his ashes were sprinkled in the Pacific Ocean. Natividad closed by telling me to light a candle in his remembrance. This was something I was already doing.

TΣM

By fall of 1977, my marriage to George Owens had broken up and I decided to purchase a small house a short distance from the one he and I had owned. At the time, I was working for the University of Cincinnati's Hoxworth Blood Center and continuing to study for my baccalaureate degree in nursing at a private women's college.

At the blood center, a co-worker told me about a psychic so I decided to make contact with her in the hopes of getting answers to those long-standing questions I had about George. The psychic made many accurate predictions but, again, there was no information regarding George.

Over the next year and an half, I would see this psychic many times. Each time I saw her, I was thinking about George but she never picked it up.

I decided to visit another psychic from Northern Kentucky but he, too, said nothing about George Reeves. I wanted someone to tell me why I always felt George was with me. I desired insight into how I had known about his death the instant it happened. Nobody could tell me. Why did I have the urge to continue this seemingly futile search? Was it even possible to know what I so hungered for?

I began meditating in an attempt to connect with George. I believed in God and the continuation of the soul after death. I knew people in the world's great religions had contacted spirits using meditative techniques. Perhaps, so could I.

During 1978, in the midst of my search for answers concerning George Reeves, I started attending a fundamentalist church. This was in part an answer to my son's request to have a more positive family atmosphere. I chose the fundamentalist church because I had been dating one of its members.

The church believed that the soul remains dead until resurrected on judgment day. According to this doctrine, once the soul is dead there is no remembrance of this life or any other previous lifetime. This belief was in direct conflict with my personal experience because I had felt George Reeves' presence, among others, at various times throughout my life. The church provided the fellowship I needed at that point in my life, so I continued to attend despite my opposing views.

The relationship that brought me to that church didn't last. Eventually, I met another man from the same church whom I married in January of 1980. His name was Duncan Cline. Duncan liked my children, loved animals, listened to music, and seemed to be a genuinely kind person. After a whirlwind courtship and marriage, life was good for a few months but that would soon change.

My ex-husband moved to Maryland to take a new job and he took our kids with him. I was now and forever to become a summer and holiday mom.

I hadn't the resources to fight for custody. I would spend the next fourteen years with the joy of their arrivals and the pain of their departures. There was never enough time to get to know them on their brief stays.

During this period, I was working on a degree in medical records in lieu of a baccalaureate degree in nursing, which I could no longer afford. I had also started working in the area of home health care, which had flexible hours allowing me to spend more time with my children during their visits. I discovered in-home nursing was a career choice that turned out to be a blessing because most nursing jobs today are in the home healthcare field.

My personal beliefs that there was life after death continued to be problematic with my church affiliation. By fall of 1987, I could no longer continue to participate in the fundamentalist church. Sending my husband alone to the services and meetings was painful but I knew deep in my soul I had made the right decision. I felt a heavy burden lifted from my spirit.

In 1985, my father died. I reflected on my father's death, the deaths of relatives, and the death of George Reeves. By this time in my professional career, I had witnessed many patients' deaths. I knew intuitively from those experiences and the experience with George Reeves that the continuation of the soul in some form was true. This knowing enabled me to give hope and consolation to my patients and their grieving families. The inner knowing that the soul survives death would be a major source of contention between Duncan and me.

TΣM

In October of 1991, I was on my way to draw blood from the only patient I had scheduled that day. It had rained the night before and the highway was covered with leaves. The route to the patient's home had several hairpin turns. As I loaded my supplies into the Trooper, a small voice inside said to be careful on those curves.

Three miles from my house, I geared down into a sharp left turn when the right wheels hit wet leaves and gravel throwing me into a skid. In an instant, the Trooper overturned. When it finally skidded to a stop, I was still buckled in the driver's seat down in a gully. I was thankful the Trooper had landed here because the opposite side was a 500-foot drop off.

This particular road was not well traveled so I wondered how long it would take someone to find me. I was hyperventilating and my left leg was pinned by the door handle and window knob. The pain was so severe I thought it might be broken. I was rational enough to turn off the engine. A small voice inside told me to unfasten my seat belt and take a deep breath. I worried that the vehicle could catch fire. Being pinned in the way I was there was no way I could open the opposite door.

After fifteen minutes a truck stopped and a man came around to my side of the vehicle asking whether I was hurt. I told him that I wasn't sure and that I couldn't move. He ran for help. I soon heard the sirens of the fire department and life squad. It took a good hour to extricate me, after which they rushed me to the nearest hospital. My admiration for paramedics increased a thousand fold that day.

After hours of x-rays and examinations, I was diagnosed with nothing more than severe bruises. I wondered why I survived and had several days to contemplate that thought. During recovery, my supervisor came to the house and discussed my future employment options. I told her I felt I could not travel for awhile and she indicated a private duty case would be opening up soon. It would be perfect because it did not require travel.

Because of my restrictions in travel, I also took a job managing a senior citizens' low-income housing facility. Working with the elderly gave me new insight and I loved it. Although I still had trouble driving in the back areas of our community, the bruises had healed and I was intent on making housing management my new career. The income was not great but, it was steady and according to my supervisor, there was room for growth. I felt working with the elderly would be where I would end my professional career.

TΣM

In January 1994, Matthew asked if he could move in with us after his graduation from college in the spring. This was because his father wanted him to get out on his own and start a life for himself. For the first time in sixteen years, I would be able to spend more time with my son. Although the relationship would not be the same as if he was a young child, I would have the opportunity to get to know him on a mature level.

In June, we rented a small van, went to Maryland and picked up Matthew. He moved into the largest spare bedroom with all his earthly belongings. He spent the days printing resumes on his computer and distributing them to prospective employers while I slept. We enjoyed going places together and he had the great ability to make me laugh. It seemed the years slowly melted away as we tried to recapture the time we had not spent together.

Matt had graduated from Howard Community College in Maryland with a degree in computer science. With a computer in the home, I decided to learn more about this new technology. Everything I had learned about computers ten years earlier was now obsolete so I started searching for an introductory course in computers at university night schools and vocational schools. That's when I picked up the fateful University of Cincinnati Communiversity catalogue and saw the parapsychology course taught by Gary Duncan. Encouraged by Matt to do something fun for a change I enrolled in Gary's class. This step would send me down a path, which would change my life forever.

Robinson Family Crypt

Identities And Past Lives

The awareness of being the witness of everything is the secret of self-realization . . .
—Sathya Sai Baba

TΣM

A Psychological & Spiritual Journey

Gary

After reviewing Jean's in-depth life history it became obvious she had been fantasy prone throughout her entire life. She was able to dissociate easily and move into fantasy worlds to escape the traumas in her life. Over time, her fantasies took on the quality of being real.

I coupled the information from Jean's life history with her current situation to get a gauge on her mental status. She had displayed an unusual trance-like state in class and had difficulty coming out of the experience. The fantasy figure George Reeves was separating from her personality becoming a distinct autonomous identity. She believed this fantasy figure was the spirit of the actor George Reeves and that he had been with her since she was a young child. In addition, she believed she and George Reeves had lived many previous lifetimes together, and on several occasions, he had taken her to alternative realities. It also appeared this fantasy figure had evolved into Jean's hero archetype, rescuing her from a dysfunctional and traumatic family environment.

An archetype is a primordial image manifesting as symbolic patterns, which emerges from the collective unconscious and can appear in many forms. In Jean's case, the archetypal form that the fantasy figure George Reeves became was a superhero character who would rescue her.

After evaluating all the information I had accumulated on Jean, I began an in-depth assessment of all the unusual behaviors and situations I had observed. I first began reviewing her disclosure regarding George Reeves in our initial clinical interview. Shortly after she disclosed the spirit of George Reeves had been with her since she was thirteen, I noticed her eyes began shifting up toward the right as if she was listening to something. I wondered whether she was hallucinating. I speculated that George Reeves was not only a delusion but possibly a hallucination as well. This prompted me to ask, "He is here isn't he?"

Jean took this to mean I was feeling George's presence along with her, but that wasn't the case at all. I was only testing a hypothesis trying to discern if she was hallucinating.

TΣM

By the second interview, I was still trying to understand the status of Jean's delusions and possible hallucinations. I continued gathering information about her mental imageries and meditations at home. She informed me the guided imageries and meditations I taught in class had changed her connections with George. She indicated George was one of her spirit guides and she communicated with him often. They had met several times in her imaginary inner room and it was there she got to know him intimately. She indicated he had taken her to this beautiful place called Coltran, and it was so beautiful she didn't want to leave.

As Jean discussed these journeys, her mood fluctuated from high anxiety to an eerie calmness. Throughout the session as in the pervious meeting, she would move her eyes up toward the right as if she was listening to something, and I assumed it was probably the George Reeves hallucination.

While watching this unusual behavior a new phenomenon surfaced. Jean's eyes shifted from right to left and then became fixed, staring trance-like in my direction. Then her eyes slightly shifted again as her facial expression changed becoming slightly sullen and somber. She spoke a few words in her usual feminine voice and then abruptly stopped.

Jean's face changed again to a sharper more pronounced masculine appearance and her voice began to quiver with anxiety. Her eyes were penetrating and flickered. Her voice became more forceful as a new identity surfaced identifying itself as George Reeves.

As I watched this, the scope to my clinical assessment broadened. I still believed she was delusional and possibly psychotic, but now she was also displaying features of Dissociative Identity Disorder commonly referred to as Multiple Personality Disorder.

As soon as this George Reeves identity emerged, I explored it. Unlike other cases of Dissociative Identity Disorder I had worked with previously, this manifestation was different. I noticed the following anomalies:

- No latency period between the emergence of the George Reeves identity and Jean's personality.
- No gaps in Jean's memory of her personal history, remote or recent.
- Jean was not in an altered state of consciousness when George emerged.
- Either personality, George or Jean could be accessed at any time.
- There were no obvious switching indicators between the emergence of George's personality and that of Jean's.
- Both personalities were in conscious awareness of the here and now.
- Both were aware of each other's emotions and thoughts.
- Each knew what the other was saying at all times.

Indicators that were usually evident with this Dissociative Identity Disorder were not present in Jean's case, and the awareness each personality had of the other was also unusual.

As George became more comfortable expressing himself through Jean, his personality became more pronounced. It was as though he was becoming a complete separate autonomous part of Jean's personality and I was able to make contact with him at any time.

When I conversed with Jean, George would just chime in whenever he had something to say. It was as though I was talking to two people sitting beside each other. Sometimes Jean would get a faraway look in her eyes when she and George were communicating with each other. I had previously believed this behavior indicated that Jean was listening to a hallucination, but as more information surfaced it was apparent she was listening to her alter personality.

I found this George Reeves identity quite interesting because there were elements in his character that indicated he had lived a separate life, totally apart from Jean. He would talk about problems he had when he was mortal and these were very different from Jean's issues.

He indicated he wanted me to help him work on those problems. Specifically, he wanted help regarding the choices he made in women. He said the women he chose to share his mortal life with were very possessive and controlling just like his mother.

The information George disclosed appeared not to fit at all with the information I had acquired on Jean's life, but I knew it had to be an intricate part of her delusional system. I felt the best way to find the answers I needed was to focus on the relationship between Jean and her alter personality George Reeves.

I asked George how long he and Jean had been together. Jean cocked her head to one side for a moment as if contemplating the question. Then George began speaking about relationships he had with women when he was alive and how bad those relationships were in comparison with the relationship he has with Jean. He indicated his relationship with Jean was very different because they are twin souls and have always been connected.

George explained when souls are created they have two opposite forces of male and female. The male and female components of Jean and George's soul decided to split apart and become twin souls. As twin souls, they could experience a variety of love relationships in a variety of incarnations. Once their two souls had experienced those love relationships they would merge back together as one soul.

George indicated all souls have this choice. Some souls choose a particular gender and stay with that gender exploring many incarnations. Other souls incarnate as either male or female to experience many lifetimes as that gender. Then that soul decides to change genders to experience many lifetimes as the opposite gender.

George explained twin souls are part of a larger spiritual picture, which includes soul mates and soul families. Soul mates are souls who have experienced many incarnations together in a close intimate relationship, but are not two parts of the same soul as with twin souls. A soul family is a group of souls who have experienced many lifetimes together, but do not have the close intimate relationship as do soul mates. All souls are connected to each other and are held together by the bonding energy of unconditional love.

George explained that when he was murdered in 1959 his soul separated from his physical body, went toward the light and connected with his spirit guide. He asked his spirit guide to find the other half of his soul. George's spirit guide took him to Jean. At the time, Jean was a thirteen-year-old girl on vacation in route to Colorado with her father and brother. George's soul then came to Jean and appeared to her in a dream. From that night on, Jean felt George's presence and intuitively knew things about his most recent life incarnation as the Superman actor George Reeves, as well as previous life incarnations.

Jean confirmed George did come to her in a dream when she was thirteen and she believed everything George said about souls was true. She said George's explanation confirmed her feelings of a connection with him. She had no doubt she and George were twin souls and had lived many lifetimes together experiencing a variety of love relationships. She indicated past-life regressions would reveal what those lifetimes were.

I was still skeptical. I felt George's explanations were his way of trying to convince me he was a separate spirit and not an alter personality. I decided to test that hypothesis by performing an experiment. I reasoned if George was a spirit then he should be able to pick up my thoughts telepathically. George agreed to do the experiment and after a few attempts, he could not pick up any of my thoughts nor could he send me any of his thoughts. His excuse was he could not get through to me psychically because I protected myself with an energy shield.

I do perform a morning ritual by putting white light around myself, but this shouldn't have kept George from perceiving my thoughts. I concluded that if George was really a spirit, he should've been able to perceive my thoughts psychically even if there was white light around me. Since he failed this simple experiment, I felt he was not a spirit but an alter personality with archetypal dimensions.

Since I was trying to understand Jean's mental status, I did not attempt to dissuade her from believing George Reeves was a spirit. I wanted to understand how this alter personality was created and what its function was. I felt by tampering with Jean's delusional system too soon that further fragmentation in her personality could occur.

I turned my attention back to the past-life regressions, in the hope of finding clues into Jean's unusual behaviors. The two regression techniques I experimented with were affect-bridge and hypnosis. The regression technique that proved to be the most effective was hypnosis. After hypnotizing Jean, I would count to three and move her back in time by ten-year intervals, and then stop and ask her what was occurring during those times. Eventually she moved back in time before her birth into this lifetime. With this method, Jean was able to recall minute details and vividly describe her experience.

I found it interesting that when I regressed Jean, George was also regressed. This was further evidence that George was not a spirit but an integral part of Jean's personality, which manifested as an alter personality. I was therefore able to obtain George's perceptions of the past-life scenarios and compare those perceptions with Jean's.

The first past-life Jean and George experienced was in the Old South during the 1840's. In this past-life, Jean and George were living on plantations in Georgia outside of Savannah. Both Jean and George's descriptions of the past-life scenes were similar except Jean described the scenes with a southern dialect and George did not.

Jean described the past-life in vivid detail. She indicated her family and George's lived on plantations situated near each other. George's family had owned their plantation for many generations unlike her family. Because the plantations were so close to each other, she and George ended up courting. Jean said George's name was John Stevens and her name was Suzanne MacIntosh in that lifetime.

Jean described the hot humid weather and the gentle breeze blowing through the trees as the hanging moss sway back and forth on the tree limbs. She detailed the slow leisurely pace of the southern lifestyle as well as conveying that her family and George's were wealthy slave owners.

Jean described how she and John would take long courtly walks in the hot summer afternoons. John was dressed in a blue-tailed coat accompanied with a short flat-topped white hat. John was the model southern gentleman and Suzanne was the elegant southern lady; they were very much in love and destined to be married.

I moved Jean two years further back in time and she described a scene in which Suzanne had been invited to a party to see John. John had been away for sometime and she desperately wanted to see him. The problem was, she needed a chaperone and at the last minute, one was finally found.

At the party, Suzanne saw John at a distance and was awe struck by his handsome appearance. To get his attention she positioned herself in the crowd so he could see her. John finally saw her in the distance looking coy. With a gleam in his eyes he made his way through the crowd, came over to her, they talked for a while and went for a short walk to be alone.

After the past-life regression was over, Jean was delighted with all the details that were surfacing. The regression scenarios were providing her with the confirmation she and George had lived in the Old South and she now believed more than ever that reincarnation is a fact.

The next past-life regression was a continuation of Jean's life in the Old South. Again, she described an idyllic picture of that lifetime just before she was married. The marriage itself went off fine with one of John's oldest and dearest friends, Robert Allen as best man. Within the first year, Suzanne became pregnant with their first child. This was to be a joyful occasion if it hadn't been for an altercation between John and Robert.

Robert was from humble beginnings and grew up with his family working for the plantation owners in the surrounding areas. Although poor, John accepted Robert as his trusted friend. As children, they played together and grew up with the feeling of being brothers.

One day John and Robert were horsing around when Robert jokingly said he would like to be in John's place and make love to Suzanne. John suddenly lost his temper and started beating Robert severely. Robert refused to fight back and was blinded in his right eye. The fight caused several other major injuries and a physician was summoned, proper medical treatment was administered and Robert slowly recovered.

The incident created a rift between John and Robert, which lasted for several years. Suzanne not knowing what the fight was about attempted on several occasions to help heal the deep wounds between the two men, but to no avail. In her attempt, she went into a deep depression and became very ill. During her illness, she gave birth to a son but he died a short time afterward. The death compounded her depression and the illness lingered for several months. As Suzanne was convalescing, John mated with a slave girl producing a daughter.

Robert kept to himself, working as a head master over the slaves in the fields on a neighboring plantation. He had heard rumors about the pregnancy of the slave girl, wanted to make contact with John, but didn't. Suzanne and John had several more children and during this period, she finally convinced him to make amends with his old friend Robert.

John eventually contacted Robert and their first meeting was very strained but cordial. The meeting was overshadowed by rumors of war because the South was asked to abolish her slave trade. John and Robert talked about states rights and the inevitability of war if the Union forced the South's hand. John indicated he would go to war if asked. Robert being blind in one eye knew he would not have to serve and had no ambition of becoming a soldier. Discussions of war created a friendly atmosphere between the two men, helping to mend their friendship by energizing them against a common foe.

It was not long before war broke out and John was called to serve in Georgia's secret militia, which eventually became part of the Confederate Army. John was elevated to First Lieutenant and shortly thereafter, made several trips home to visit Suzanne and the children. On his last visit, John contacted Robert and indicated that, although their friendship had been strained, he still trusted him when it came to his family. He asked Robert to keep in close contact with Suzanne and the children, making sure they were safe and well supplied in his absence.

After the visit, John took another command in the Confederate Army. His letters to Suzanne were very sparse and gave no indication where he was. The months were long and turned into a year without Suzanne, the family, or Robert ever seeing John again.

One hot autumn day Suzanne received a letter from the Confederate Army telling her John had been killed in a battle near Chickamauga outside of Chattanooga, Tennessee. Shortly after Suzanne received the letter, Robert showed up to report on their food supplies. With tears streaming down her cheeks, she handed Robert the letter. He read it with a lack of expression, handed the letter back to Suzanne, turned and walked away.

Robert walked over to a large Magnolia tree, sat under it and began reflecting on the friendship he had had with John. One memory that flashed through his mind was John teaching him how to read when they were children. Now the words John had taught him so long ago leaped from the letter, settling in his mind, carrying the message that John was dead.

Robert stayed on at the plantation, managing the daily functions making sure Suzanne and the family were safe and well supplied. As the war continued, it took its toll on Suzanne. Not only did she lose John to the war but she also lost her two young sons. Shortly after hearing about her sons' deaths, Suzanne fell ill from consumption and died a few years later in 1866.

I found it interesting how Jean was able to get into the inner experiences of Suzanne, John and Robert and relay the details vividly. I was struck with how well Jean had weaved together the life stories of these past-life characters. The vivid details she used in describing these past-lives prompted me to investigate other past-lives.

I regressed Jean back to her death as Suzanne in 1866, and slowly brought her forward searching for other lifetimes she might have lived. I counted the years forward allowing Jean to drift slowly through each one. She abruptly stopped at a lifetime toward the end of the nineteenth century.

The past-life regression scene opened with Jean and George who were now brother and sister on a train heading for their new home in Iowa. A farm family had adopted them from an orphanage. Jean and her brother ended up in the orphanage after their parents died suddenly.

Jean was about seven years old and her brother was much younger. She was his protector and felt somewhat like a parent. The train ride to Iowa was very rough and in route the train derailed and Jean and her brother were killed. Jean expressed sadness over this lifetime because it was so short.

TΣM

After the past-life regressions, I attempted to understand Jean's experiences clinically. Once again, I reviewed her personal history focusing on all the tragedies in her life, her ease to become fantasy prone, her ability to dissociate into trance-like experiences and her alter personality who had become her hero archetype. I felt Jean used these experiences as coping strategies.

Even Jean's past-lives functioned as an explanation for her tragic life. These past-life scenarios reflected her personal history, which was fraught with many tragedies, including the death of her mother, an unemotional and controlling father, the death of her grandmother, and having to step into the parent role to help raise her brother. These tragedies continued with a failed marriage in which Jean had to give up her children to her ex-husband because of her financial situation.

These early tragedies allowed Jean to take refuge into her fantasy world. In this fantasy world, her hero figure George Reeves would rescue her any time she needed. Eventually this hero figure took on a variety of archetypal dimensions besides being her rescuer. He became her lover, teacher, guide, advisor and soul companion.

These tragedies coupled with Jean's tendency toward fantasy appeared to create her intricate delusional system. Within this delusional system, Jean created the past-life scenarios to explain her connection with the actor George Reeves. She further elaborated this delusion by creating a spiritual bond with him in which they were twin souls.

Not only had Jean created an elaborate delusional system but also she had created a fantasy world that could be described vividly. As Jean elaborated on her experiences in both Coltran and the past-life scenarios, I was amazed with all the intricate details she could describe.

Although Jean was describing her inner experience, I knew I was not getting the complete picture. There were perceptual nuances I was not privy to. I knew she was keeping a diary and wondered how her diary descriptions differed from what she was telling me.

Jean's visits to Coltran as well as her past-lives convinced her that she and George Reeves were twin souls and had lived many lifetimes together. From the past-life scenarios, it was clear Jean believed deeply in reincarnation, and the past-life regressions proved she and George had lived many lifetimes together.

I, on the other hand, do not equate past-life scenarios with reincarnation; these two concepts are very different.

A remembered past-life in a regression is a symbolic representation of what is occurring in the person's current lifetime. These past-lives are strictly archetypal and metaphorical and are not to be taken literally. Ian Stevenson at the University of Virginia has researched reincarnation memories and they appear to be present within the first few years of life, shortly after birth. Based on his research, I believe reincarnation memories are not accessed through past-life regressions.

What I perceived Jean to be experiencing in her regressions were archetypal past-life memories and not reincarnation memories. Jean on the other hand, was convinced that she and George Reeves have gone through many incarnations together. I perceived this belief to be part of an elaborate delusional system Jean had constructed as a coping mechanism.

TΣM

    As I was attempting to sort through and make sense of all the information I had collected on Jean she made an unusual request. She asked if I would meet her in my office on the anniversary date and time of the George Reeves' death. I thought this was a rather odd request given the short time we had been working together. I quickly surmised, since she had taken several of my classes, and was now my client, she probably thought our relationship was on a friendlier basis. I felt since her ego boundaries were diffused it was easy for her to make such an inappropriate request.

    I asked Jean why she wanted me to meet her at my office on that date. She indicated George had informed her something very profound was going to happen and we needed to be together to experience it. I was very reluctant to agree with her request, especially after checking my schedule to discover June 16th would be a Sunday. I told her I would have to think about it and left it at that.

The Unveiling of a Tragedy

For many men that stumble at the threshold are well foretoldthat danger lurks within . . .
—Shakespeare (Henry VI)

TΣM

Tuesday April 30, 1996

Today George told me the major screw-up in my life was that I was supposed to have been his daughter this time around to complete our reincarnation cycle, whatever that means. He indicated he and his wife Eleanor could not have children and my soul went somewhere else to be born into another family. I was amazed such mistakes could be made on a spiritual level. George said some things in a lifeline were unchangeable, but others could be altered, such as the parents a soul chooses to incarnate with. He spent a lot of time trying to help me understand my life's journey and why things happened the way they did. It was odd to think I am someone I possibly should not have been.

After our discussion about soul reincarnation, George indicated he wanted me to get in touch with Jack Larson. Jack was the only remaining close friend who could recognize George. George has things he wants Jack to know and I am not sure what they are at this point.

Monday May 6, 1996

The past few days were uneventful. I had a cold and George has been letting me rest more. I know he is there by the usual feelings of his arms around me. He quietly urges me to rest and I drift into an almost dreamless sleep. I awakened knowing I have dreamed but have no memory of what the dreams were.

During the morning before our session, George was very talkative and I knew he would say a lot to Gary. He informed me when we were all together during the plantation days, Gary was an overseer of the slaves on the plantation next to ours. Gary was always jovial and would talk with us for hours after the day's work was done. We would have cakes and coffee and I would always surprise Gary with little gifts.

Because Gary had no wife, he enjoyed our family atmosphere immensely. During the Civil War, he provided moral support to our family after John was killed in battle. Whatever relationship I had with Gary in the past has helped me trust him in the present. Because of that past-life relationship, I find it easy to talk with Gary on the most personal of subjects.

In today's regression, I went into the trance easily and Gary took me back to the plantation at a time before the war. In the scene, John and I had two teenage sons. At the time, he belonged to the secret Georgia Militia and eventually went off to war. John was in his early fifties and was getting too old to be in the regular military units, although the South seemed to take all able-bodied men after a certain point in the war.

After the regression, George talked with Gary awhile, telling him about the mistake in my birth parentage. George also revealed that both of my children were his; Matt was more like him and Amy more like her biological father. There is an undeniable resemblance between George and Matthew both physically and in their personalities.

Wednesday May 8, 1996

During today's meditation, George took me to the most beautiful place I have ever experienced called Coltran. This is where our home is located on the spiritual plane. Our house was on a beach much like the condominium on St. Simon's Island, Georgia. The sky was a purplish color and the grass was a yellow-green. A steady breeze blew that I could actually feel with a sweet fragrance on its currents.

Throughout the community were walkways made of materials that looked like stone, but had a rubberized give to it as you walked. Lining the walkways were gaslights with flames of a crimson red. People were riding in small vehicles, similar to hovercrafts but powdered with something called Universal Power.

I saw a variety of people from light brown to bronze and white. Some were communicating by telepathic transmission and others used a spoken language that was unfamiliar. Everyone understood each other and everyone understood English. I had an immense feeling of peace and a deep connection to all the people.

The people were dressed predominately in white robe-type tops with flowing shirts and slacks. The clothes were unisex and worn by both men and women, the only difference were the color of sashes and jeweled decorations. The men's sashes were darker in color. They wore moccasins.

The leaves on the trees were exquisite pinks and blues and textured like velvet. George informed me the fruit on these trees was edible and anyone could come and gather them. The society was vegan so most of the flowers and bushes produced edible fruits and vegetables, and in some cases, the entire plant was edible.

The buildings were adobe, tan and white. Our home was white with turquoise accents on the doors, windows, and along back porches. It was two stories. Both levels overlooked the beautiful ocean of turquoise water, which was almost the exact color of the house's trim. George told me the water was so sweet you could drink it. The beaches were white sand, soft and comfortable.

The houses used spring water for personal use and many of the homes were built directly over the springs. The springs were also used to irrigate the growing areas in the lower levels of the houses where the residents could produce their own food.

Throughout Coltran, there were entertainment centers for music, plays, and non-competitive games. The place was so beautiful and peaceful I didn't want to leave. George said this was our place of rest and we will have our honeymoon here; it was to be our permanent base. Who could be afraid to die when a place like this exists?

I was back in my living room and had only been away for an hour and a half.

Friday May 10, 1996

It was a perfect day to drive the scenic route along the Ohio River to Rising Sun, Indiana. I hadn't been to this area for over a year. The city had petitioned for a gambling boat, so the quaintness will soon disappear. I went to my favorite spot to meditate, a public park along the river. Even during late morning there were only two other people in the park. It was sunny and the light danced off the river as if gold coins were being tossed in the air.

The summer birds were back and some were darting into the waves to catch bugs or small fish. The road across the river in Rabbit Hash, Kentucky was not busy and where I was sitting seemed far enough away to make the houses and cars appear smaller than life. The park was a wonderful place to get in touch with my feelings and relax from the weekly grind.

I sat quietly gazing at the river in the warm morning sun, and soon drifted into meditation.

I was back at our home in Coltran.

This time George took me inside the house. The color scheme was much like the outside, white, beige, and turquoise. The rooms were large, airy and filled with sunlight. We passed through the kitchen, dining room, and living room. I noticed oak furniture and many shelves of books.

I caught a brief glimpse of the balcony off the front of the living room just before we ascended the staircase. We made a left turn and entered the bedroom located over the living room with the same dimensions. The furniture was shaker style. Everything was simple and natural.

We laid on the bed for a short time and it felt like lying on a cloud with the sounds of the ocean echoing through the house. George hadn't said much to me at that point. He had just led me to the bed smiling his wonderful warm smile and then asked if I liked our home. I could only nod my head yes, because a large lump of emotion was caught in my throat. With the love radiating from his face, I realized he would do anything in his power to make me happy.

As quickly as I had gone to that wonderful place, I was propelled back to this reality when I heard a car door closing. There were tears of happiness in the corners of my eyes and I wiped them away not to appear sad. George asked if I had enjoyed my visit and I emphatically replied, "Yes." This experience made me want to be with him even more.

The one consolation I have is the place we will be together after my death is the most peaceful place I have ever been.

Saturday May 11, 1996

It was class day again and the experience I was having was like being in two realities at the same time. I know that sounds strange but I had a strong feeling George was trying to take me back and forth between the two realities. I told Matt during the first class period, I was feeling strange.

In the second half of class, we went into a meditation as usual. I warned Gary during break something might happen in the meditation and I even asked Matt to help me if necessary. Gary used a gong to take us into the meditation and during the experience he wanted us to go where our spirit led us. Gary had no idea where the spirit of George Reeves was going to take me, and, having cart-blanche, George was going to take full advantage of the situation.

George took me back to Coltran, but instead of going to the house, we went to the beach, boarded one of the small hovercrafts, and went to a lovely little island. George said it was a lover's vacation spot. The sand was the same pristine white as on the mainland and the ocean reflected a clear and turquoise hue. He took my hand and we waded into the comfortable cool water.

There were strange yellow fish swimming around our legs and George explained they were edible. They have a cartilage edge that can be peeled away, and the meat cooked in one piece. We walked back onto the beach toward a stand of trees. The foliage was brightly colored and George indicated the fruit was edible tasting like a peach.

A loud gong startled me and I gasped at being flung from one reality into another.

After coming out of the meditation, Gary had us stand and shake our arms and stomp our feet to re-ground ourselves. I talked to Gloria who was sitting beside me and realized something was not right in my thinking. I could not focus on what Gary and Gloria were saying. Gary was asking questions of the class but all I could hear was a mumble. I knew George was with me because I could feel his arms holding me tight and saying Gary would have to bring me out of the trance. It was as though part of my awareness was with George and part with the class. I couldn't move or say anything; I felt paralyzed.

When the class ended, Matt tried to bring me back to waking reality but couldn't. Gary gave us a concerned look but was busy with other students. After the other students left, Gary sat next to me and I heard him tell Matt and Gloria that I might be channeling. He then asked if George was with me. All I could do was to nod yes.

After about a minute, George explained to Gary he needed to count me out of the trance the way he does in his office. Gary first tried to count me out of the trance but I remained in the reverie and could not respond to his voice. He took me by the hand and led me out into the hallway away from Matt and Gloria. Looking into my eyes, he counted me deeper into the trance and then counted me back out. At that point, something released and I was back to conscious reality, but felt like I had just awakened from a dream.

Gary, Matt, and I talked for a few minutes mostly to convince Matt that I was okay. To alleviate Matt's concern, Gary suggested I should set a timer so I would have a startle sound to bring me back to conscious reality when I meditate at home. Although Matt was concerned I would not come out of a trance, I was not worried because George was in control and I knew he would take care of me.

Later that evening George brought up a new subject during my pre-work rest. He told me he wanted the three of us to get together on the anniversary date of his death, June 16, only five weeks away. I had the feeling something big was going to happen and I hoped Gary could be with us on that night because he might get some insights into what happened to George the night he died.

Monday May 13, 1996

During session today, we first established Gary had to bring me out of the meditation in class the way he does in session by counting me out. The past Saturday in class, I was in an altered state before the meditation and that was why the gong didn't return me to waking reality.

Gary and George talked throughout the session about George's guilt feelings concerning his life when he was alive and about our previous lifetime together on the plantation. A most interesting detail emerged concerning Gary's past-life connection with me on the plantation after John had died.

Gary's name in that past-life was Robert Allen and he was very important to our family. I would not have survived during and after the war if it weren't for his help. I felt there was definitely an emotional bond between us. George told Gary he was important to us here in the present and had waited until the time was right to set things up between us all. The karmic link among us had to be completed during this lifetime. George also indicated if the three of us had reconnected earlier in this lifetime I would not have married Duncan.

As George continued to speak through me, it was as though I was sitting backstage listening to him and Gary talk. The information that came out of my mouth was nothing I was aware of, had even thought of, or had heard before. I could sense George's personality and could distinguish his from mine.

At the end of the session, Gary asked George to step aside so I could regain my composure. It was odd to feel that sometimes George wanted to continue talking and not let me return. At other times, he allowed me to return quickly because he did not want to say anything more on a particular topic or just wanted to think about it for a while.

TΣM

After I had returned, Gary asked about the place George had taken me to Saturday in class. I gave some details about Coltran and Gary indicated it sounded like a place another person, who'd had a near death experience, had described to him. I then told Gary that George wanted us to get together on June 16th and Gary seemed interested but wanted to think about it first.

TΣM

George is usually very talkative after our sessions with Gary. Sometimes it's about questions Gary has asked and sometimes it's about memories the session triggers. The session today triggered George's wish for me to get in touch with Jack Larson because he really didn't like the image that *Unsolved Mysteries* portrayed of him. George said the house layout was all wrong, the way he died was wrong, and Jack had changed his story about George's mental condition during that time. Jack was the only one left who could be convinced George was back.

George said he could tell me many things about his relationship with Jack and would be able to speak to him through me the way he does when talking with Gary. This may even convince Jack that George is here. The whole thing frightens me a bit because I am a private person and don't know what the publicity would do to my life.

Tuesday May 14, 1996

I awoke at noon, ecstatic with George nuzzling and talking to me when a strange thing happened. My inner awareness quickly shifted and I found myself in Gary's office. He was wearing a beige shirt with a banded collar, and appeared to be in deep thought. He got up, walked over to his desk, sat down, and started looking through a small ledger.

I stood behind Gary placing my hands on his shoulders and could hear the music he plays in the background during our sessions. He looked up as if he sensed a presence, got up from his desk and walked to the bookcase. As quickly as it had happened, I was back in my bed again.

I remembered Gary had said it was possible to travel out of body during ecstatic experiences if you focus on it first, but this was spontaneous. Was this a new experience George wanted me to have? He had certainly created the conditions for it to occur. I would have to find out on Monday when I see Gary if he was in his office at that time.

Thursday May 16, 1996

Today George took me back to Coltran. He seems to enjoy taking me there. Maybe he feels like he's an intruder in my home because of Duncan. This time we were dressed in off-white tunics with colored scarves and sashes. George told me the red sash I was wearing indicated I was a visitor.

We entered our home through a side door into the kitchen. Upon entering, there was a short split stairway, leading down to a hydroponic garden. The upper stairs led into a most beautiful working area with red oak storage cabinets. The sink was white marble. On the work island there were turquoise glazed tiles. Although the room was at the back of the house it was still bright and cheerful.

We then walked through the kitchen area into the dining room and there in the center was a large oval rosewood table. It was so highly polished it appeared to be wet. Surrounding the table were comfortable-looking, high-backed chairs upholstered in a beige fabric.

There was a flower centerpiece sitting elegantly on the table with a variety of brilliant colors. George laughed and told me to go over and touch them, which I did. To my surprise they were real. He indicated he always kept fresh flowers there just for me because he knows how much I love them.

The china closet held crystal, which gleamed in the sun creating rainbows on the opposite wall. George gently put his arm around my waist and escorted me into the living room. There were pictures of seascapes aligning the walls to my left and right. Straight ahead was a wall of windows that looked out onto the ocean from a balcony running the entire width of the house. As I looked around at this beauty, I was almost breathless with the magnificence of it all. George grinned and asked if I had forgotten something. Upon saying that, he pushed a button and the entire glass panel moved making outside vista part of the room. The smells, the sounds, and the breeze were right in the room. It was heaven!

I turned away from this lovely vista to gaze at the rest of the room. A large white curved sectional sofa with blue pillows dominated the room. The wall beyond was covered with built-in bookcases filled with books. To my left was a multi-media viewer and on the wall were lovely paintings of other places.

George took my hand and guided me out of the room, up the stairs, and into our bedroom. He then escorted me to the two other large bedrooms at the back of the house, each with a bath. One of the bedrooms obviously was done in a masculine decor of dark wood and red accessories. The other bedroom was more feminine with softer and lighter colors. He said he would tell me about those rooms later and led me back into our bedroom.

We took a shower in a large cylinder encloure, which was used only as a washing and refreshing area. George explained the reason there were no commodes was that food burned so efficiently in the body there was no waste. We used a wonderful woodsy smelling herbal soap that left my skin feeling soft and tingly.

After we towel dried, words could not describe the ecstasy of the time we spent together. It was over too soon, and at the peak of the experience I was catapulted back into this reality. I could feel him curled up to me and he asked if I was happy. I think the tears of joy were the only answer I could give. I was loved!

TΣM

It was a beautiful day, so Matt, Duncan, and I took a family trip to the tourist town of Metamora, Indiana, with its artist and craft shops. I used to do home health visits in the area so it brought back many memories. The town grew up around the small remaining section of the old Miami-Whitewater canal, which used to join the Ohio branch of the Erie Canal.

In the town, there is an old historic working gristmill adding to the picturesque scene. The remaining canal section stretches about a mile out of town with a small roadside park outfitted with picnic tables. When I was working in the area as a nurse and when time permitted, I would eat my lunch there.

Walking through the various stores and shops, we ended up in a Native American establishment and I could feel George immediately liking the place. He had me purchase an Indian herbal charm bag to ward off evil influences. George said it would come in handy in the future and would tell me how to use it later. I immediately knew he was talking about the spirits of Eddie and Toni Mannix.

The sales clerk told me to add a personal talisman to the bag when I got home and I knew just what that would be. I had a lovely rose quartz crystal and an amethyst and knew they would fit perfectly in the bag. It occurred to me I had never seen such a good luck charm locally and knew it had to be something George wanted me to have.

After the trip, George informed me to be easy on Duncan because he was not as quick to comprehend things and tended to forget easily. George said I look at people as if they have equal ability, which was good, but sometimes I forget people's limitations. We Libras like harmony and I'm no exception.

Monday May 20, 1996

After the trip to Metamora, I had a full night's sleep so I was more alert than usual for my session with Gary. In the session, George was still insisting that I contact Jack Larson. I said meeting Jack frightens me a bit because of the publicity. Gary said Jack puts his pants on one leg at a time just as we do. George said he'd be with me to take the edge off any encounter.

Gary and I spoke briefly about my spirit visit to his office and he confirmed he had been wearing the same shirt I had seen. I then realized I had actually been in his office! After that disclosure, Gary hypnotized me again and took me back to the plantation.

During the regression, John and the children were absent and I knew they were dead. I then realized after their deaths Robert Allen cared for and protected me from the carpetbaggers and other marauders combing the area during and after the war. All my known family was either dead or missing because of the war's devastation. The stress and personal losses due to the war were so severe my health was compromised and I died from consumption in 1866.

Gary then moved me forward to the next lifetime George and I shared together. We were brother and sister living in an orphanage in Illinois just before the turn of the century. We were on a train trip with other orphans heading to Iowa. In route, the train wrecked killing us both. My name in that lifetime was Annie. George's name was Donny.

After the regression, Gary asked George if there were more past lives to come. George replied there were none because soon thereafter he was born in this lifetime in 1914. He also indicated in this lifetime I should have been his daughter and that would have completed the cycle of love.

Through all the lifetimes George and I have lived, we have been husband and wife, or brother and sister. In this incarnation, we were to be father and daughter, but there was a change in our reincarnation situation. The whole theme of our existence has been to learn what love relationships can bring.

George says these love relationships are the entire key to human experiences. We humans need to know about various types of love experiences so we can recreate them repeatedly until we remember what love is truly about.

Wednesday May 22, 1996

Today I finally had time to meditate again. I settled into my relaxation mode and asked George to take me anywhere he would like. Usually it is Coltran but this time it was different. He took me to a sound stage on the Superman set and I immediately realized it was the last experience George had on the set just before he died. He was wearing an open collar white sports shirt and a beige jacket. He greeted many people who appeared to be evaluating the sets. There were many greetings, handshakes, and slaps on the back from his co-workers.

The mood on the set was happy but I sensed there was a bit of hesitation on George's part. Even though he said nothing was wrong, there was still that cautious feeling emanating from him. He told a few of the set technicians about the upcoming exhibition with Archie Moore and he threw a few shoulder punches in jest. One man kidded him about his fighting weight, which was a little on the heavy side.

A make-up artist took George aside to look at the scar on his forehead resulting from a car accident in Benedict Canyon. Although the wound had healed, George was still concerned about close-ups. He indicated he didn't want plastic surgery but would consider it if there were problems down the road. George then walked over to Jack Larson, who was sitting near a stairway, and Jack greeted him warmly. George kidded him about playing a hand or two of poker as he pulled a deck of cards from his pocket. It seemed card playing was a common pastime between set ups. Jack told George he would be happy to play a game of poker after he saw Whitney the producer.

The scene closed and I was back in my living room with George and he said matter-of-factly, "There—that proves I was ready to go back to work to start a new project. I wasn't depressed. But I was looking for something else to do in my life."

I could relate to that because it seems the forties are a time of rethinking about your life, no matter what you are doing, or how successful you are.

Saturday May 25, 1996

In class today, Gary looked pale and weak. He told us he had been passing kidney stones all week and was still having pain. As a nurse, I felt he should have stayed home in bed drinking lots of cranberry juice and water. There is such a thing as being too dedicated to one's work.

In the class meditation, George took me back to 1860. John and I were taking a trip to Savannah in a beautiful black Phaeton Carriage pulled by a chestnut mare. We were going to see our tobacco and cotton agent to sell the season's harvest, then visit an aunt and uncle, and then go shopping. Along the way, I saw the dusty red roadway and felt a gentle breeze caress me. It was early morning and we talked about the good time we would have in the city. I didn't get a chance to shop often so I was very excited.

In route, we stopped by the neighboring plantation and talked with our friend Robert about a secret militia and the coming war. The subject matter became upsetting and I was anxious to get away from the war talk. We stopped a bit further down the road, sat under a tree and ate a picnic lunch of ham, fruit and tea, which had been packed for us.

We were just about to enter the outskirts of Savannah when the gong sounded. I heard it but did not return to the classroom mentally. I soon heard Gary counting me out of the meditation and found myself back in class. I wondered if some of my difficulty in returning was because I really didn't want to return at that moment. I also think sometimes George wants to show me more than time allows.

Gary lectured about setting up a protective energy field around our personal space. A protective barrier so unwanted energies could not get in and drain our energy during meditation. Gary told the class he creates a protective barrier around himself most of the time to keep his energy from being drained. He also indicated many people can feel the barrier around him and cannot get emotionally close for that reason. I haven't felt the barrier and wondered if it was because of our previous incarnation.

At the end of class, I gave Gary a video of the *Unsolved Mysteries* program. I hoped the video would give Gary a better idea of what happened on June 16, 1959.

Monday May 27, 1996

In session, Gary and I talked about my meditation experience in class in which George and I were heading to Savannah, Georgia. Since the gong interrupted the experience, Gary decided to regress me back to that time. Instead of the regression scene opening with John and me traveling to Savannah, it opened to my fatal illness after the Civil War.

I was with Robert Allen and could feel much emotion because I was dying of complications from consumption, referred to now as tuberculosis. I felt the tightness in my chest. It was difficult to breathe. It felt like being smothered. This explained my present life's fear of suffocating.

Robert meant a lot to me because of his help around the plantation after my husband John had been killed in the Civil War. He protected me. During this time it was very dangerous for women to be alone.

As I relived the experience, I felt no pain upon dying. I floated first into darkness and then toward a light where I returned to John. John told me we would all be together again soon.

Gary halted the regression and brought me forward in time to the Illinois orphanage. I was seven and George was nine. The orphanage personnel abused me for my intuition. As in the previous regression, we were on a train heading for Iowa to be adopted by a farm family when the train derailed and we were killed. At that point, Gary terminated the regression because he didn't want me to experience dying two times in one session. Gary said we'd visit that experience next time.

Once back, Gary talked with George for a while about Coltran. George again mentioned love was the key to our entire existence and if we could just learn how to love and live by it, life would be more meaningful.

Saturday June 1, 1996

It was a quiet week so Matt and I decided to go to an oldies concert sponsored by one of the local radio stations. I felt George was with us. He later said he enjoyed the concert but it was more for my generation than his. George likes big band music, which allows people to dance closely. I could feel his arms around me as he nuzzled in my ear when he heard a romantic song. He was happy Matt and I had a good time and said I should do it more often because he feels I'm a workaholic and do not take enough time to relax.

Monday June 3, 1996

Tonight at work I felt I connected with Gary again. There were several issues on his mind and the feelings were so overwhelming I knew I had penetrated his psychic space. I decided I would ask him about this.

Gary later confirmed my feelings. He told me the psychological barriers must be coming down between us, which also meant that George would be getting through to him as well. Gary said he had decided to meet me at the office on the anniversary of George's death on June 16th but I felt he was still somewhat reluctant. George was very happy about Gary's decision and was almost smug about it, as if he knew it was going to happen anyway.

Tuesday June 4, 1996

During meditation, George took me to Spring Grove Cemetery and shockingly, I saw a headstone with my name and the date of my death on it, December 1996. I meditated on the meaning of this. Then I felt an urgency, as if something unfinished beckoned for attention. I was puzzled!

Later that day, Gary regressed me again back to the orphanage. He felt this past-life was not as detailed as my other past-life experiences and wondered if there was something in the death experience preventing those details from emerging.

It was 1896. My brother and I boarded the train. The train trip and the prospect of new parents didn't seem to worry me. It all felt like a great adventure.

As more details emerged, I could smell the acrid sulfur as it billowed from the train engine's pipe. The trip was underway and I soon fell asleep.

Out of nowhere, there was a crash and Donny was tossed over me. We were both critically injured and died quickly. I felt myself being pulled into a light and soon Donny and I were reunited with Robert, who had died some fifteen years earlier.

On a conscious level, I realized we were in Coltran.

We discussed our next incarnation. Donny said I would come back as his daughter so we could learn to love in a very different way. We had experienced marital love and sibling love. Next we needed to know the love of parent and child.

As we talked, there was a sudden shift in my awareness. I had been brought forward in time and was alone with Robert. I realized Donny had been reincarnated into a man named George Reeves. Other spirits in Coltran were discussing what was going to happen in their next incarnation. I felt there was some reason I didn't want to go back to the way things were planned and at that point, Gary shifted the focus to George. I could feel George's presence as Gary returned him back to the 1860's.

In the regression, George revealed John and Robert had an intimate relationship in their adolescence and that Robert had been jealous of the relationship between John and Suzanne. To maintain this intimate relationship with John, Robert wanted to become part of the relationship between John and Suzanne. This created a dilemma, which eventually lead to a fight between Robert and John.

Gary later indicated he had always had a feeling of dislike toward George Reeves and could not stomach the Superman TV series. Gary indicated it was never the character per se, but the actor. Gary said he had no idea why he felt that way, prompting George to point out it was probably due to the altercation they had in their previous incarnation together. Then George spoke briefly about the Hollywood system; how it warped your thinking and literally took over your life.

Before leaving the office, I gave Gary an old collector's record of James Dean playing the bongos. Gary had exhibited some interest in Dean and I thought he might enjoy the record. I found it during spring cleaning and George said he thought Gary would like it also. Gary seemed pleased and said he would frame it and put it in his den. I also told Gary I thought his negative feelings toward George probably prevented George from getting through to him telepathically and for him to consider that possibility.

A Psychological & Spiritual Journey

Wednesday June 6, 1996

I went into a meditation and discovered more information regarding the relationship between George and Gary on the plantation. Robert not only had feelings for John, but he also had them for me. He desired an intimate relationship with both of us. John could not deal with sharing me and started a fight with Robert in which he beat him severely. This occurred shortly after John and I had married.

After the incident, John wept over what he had done to his best friend. This was the first time I had been truly angry with John. To help mend the wounds, I nursed Robert back to health in our home and this created deep feelings toward him on my part.

Though John eventually reconciled with Robert, he spent the rest of his life being contrite for the injuries he had caused him. As part of the reconciliation, John gave Robert many books. Robert was a voracious reader. John also secretly subsidized Robert's subsequent pay raise on the plantation where he worked.

TΣM

Later in the day, George insisted I call Gary about the book he wants us to write. The theme is still unclear to me, but George is intent on me looking for biographical information. This research would possibly include me going to Galesburg, Illinois.

George's book idea was spiritual. George says if we could get the details right it would certainly be a bestseller. A collaboration among the three of us would be the best way to proceed because each has information the other doesn't.

George tried to psychically contact Gary but failed. This prompted George to contact Gary's spirit guide, Little Bear, to try to make the connection work. George has a spirit guide named White Eagle who could collaborate with Little Bear. George feels we must renew our psychic connection for the book project to proceed. If I have learned anything in the last two months it's George knows the timing for what should be done and when. I just need to have more faith in his direction.

Monday June 10, 1996

Gary talked with George most of the session today. He was interested in George's movies and his relationships with various actresses as well as with Toni and Eddie Mannix. George said if a situation presented itself with an actress on a movie set and if there was mutual interest he would take advantage of the situation. This all ended when he became involved with Toni Mannix.

George and Toni met earlier at a cast party when he was making *Gone With The Wind*. At the time, George was involved with Eleanor Needles and soon to be married, so the situation never developed with Toni. After his divorce from Eleanor, he and Toni met at a Hollywood party. This time Toni pursued him.

At another event sometime later, George was taken aside by Eddie Mannix, Toni's husband. At the event, Eddie told George, Toni was interested in him sexually and if he submitted to her interest, it would be worthwhile professionally.

According to Eddie, he claimed to be impotent because of heart medication and wanted George to service Toni. This alliance would keep Toni happy and content and would allow Eddie to pursue his own separate interests. Toni was a very attractive woman, eight years George's senior and George saw the career benefits in this new forged collaboration. This was the beginning of a situation, which would eventually lead to George's death.

After George disclosed his connection with Eddie and Toni Mannix, Gary regressed me again to the early 1860's. Gary was interested in knowing what we looked like physically in that lifetime. I was 5'4" with long black curly hair with dark eyes. John was 5'10" with black hair, mustache, beard, and expressive blue eyes. In the earlier regressions, I perceived John's eyes as being dark but in this regression his eyes were blue and I found that small change in detail quite interesting. Robert Allen was 5'7" with brown hair and gray eyes, which had a golden speckle. Robert wore a mustache with a red cast to it. It appeared our appearances have not changed much throughout the various incarnations.

After the regression, I felt disoriented so Gary insisted I sit for awhile to regain my composure before leaving his office. While resting we discussed the June 16th meeting and George indicated it would be important for the book. I also told Gary that Matt would be interested in attending the meeting, from both a curiosity standpoint and for propriety, because 4 a.m. was a rather unusual hour to meet, especially on a Sunday.

Tuesday June 11, 1996

George woke me up in a loving embrace with words of encouragement. Even on the most trying of days the experience with him makes me remember we are part of a grander picture.

Later in the afternoon during meditation, I told George to take me anywhere he wanted to go. First, he took me to Gary's office and Gary was sitting at his desk talking on the telephone. We departed Gary's office leaving good feelings for him so he'd have an uplifting day.

The next stop on our spiritual journey was somewhere we had never gone before. George said it was the third star, second planet in a galaxy but didn't name which one. The planet had a very arid climate and felt much like our southwest, and was inhabited by two races of people. One race was red-skinned with short black hair. They had a singsong spoken language, much like the East Indians. Their written language was similar to Persian. They also communicated telepathically.

I did not see much of the living spaces but our room had cool shades of green and blue. The cooling effect of the colors was to offset the harsh dry climate. I was aware there was a third sex and three person alliances were common.

The other race was possibly the space men so often described in UFO reports. They were tall and had a pearl white cast to their skin with little or no hair. One had what looked like gray fuzz on his head and maybe that was an indicator of gender. In their communication with each other, one said they were looking for "the old genes." They had been to Earth in earlier years and were returning to find this genetic material. They had been experimenting on combining races genetically for durability and were now looking for the primary gene structure.

In our culture, medical science is moving into the area of gene manipulation and genetic therapies. Maybe it was started a long time ago by this race of beings. That would explain why there have been surges of UFO sightings throughout history. Maybe they are returning to gather data on previous experiments just as we do in our labs. I also got the impression the gray-skinned people were not original inhabitants of the planet and had not bred with the indigenous people. The planet was a way station to other galactic planetary systems.

I returned to my living room after a journey of about forty-five minutes and who knows how many light-years. I had asked George to show me other realities but never dreamed I would see anything so dramatic. It seems once George and I visit a place we usually return to it. We have gone to Coltran several times and I expect I will see this arid planet once again. Maybe we all are space travelers but just don't know it.

Friday June 14, 1996

George and I have been anticipating the meeting in Gary's office Sunday June 16th. I have also been feeling vaguely depressed and wonder if it's connected with the anniversary of George's death. George has been loving but I sense a bit of anxiety on his part. I feel he is preparing me for what I will be experiencing on Sunday because I feel his presence more acutely now. I get a sense of being embraced, pressure around my torso like arms encircling, a tickling sensation on the side of my face and occasionally pressure on my lips like a kiss.

I feel the experience in Gary's office will be distressing so I decided to warn Matthew. As always, I am thinking about the events that led up to that day thirty-seven years ago. It will seem strange to have my memory of the experience along with George's.

I have been unable to get George to try to connect with Gary psychically for the last three or four days. He says he won't leave me at this time because of the upcoming meeting. I feel our bond getting stronger.

Sunday June 16, 1996

The day has finally arrived and George woke me up at 2 a.m. He was holding me tight and weeping and said he was sorry to put me through this experience. Because George loves me so deeply he doesn't really want me to see all that happened that night but knows it will be necessary for the truth to be known.

I woke Matt up and shortly thereafter we were on our way to Gary's office. I told Matt he could either watch what happens or stay in the waiting room, whatever he wished. Matt and I didn't talk much on the way, but I was acutely aware of George's presence.

Arriving at the office building, Gary's truck was already in the parking lot. He had just arrived and was preparing his cup of coffee when we entered the office. After preliminary greetings, we went into Gary's counseling room and I took my customary place on the couch. Matt stood in the doorway because he had not come to a firm decision about whether to watch or not.

Gary wondered if he would have to try to hypnotize George through me to get him back to that time in California, but that wasn't necessary. George took over my body immediately and, with a brief prompting from Gary, George took the lead. Gary asked George about the game he played where he'd fire an unloaded gun at his temple. George informed Gary it had started while he was in the service during the war and he did this to reduce stress.

George explained the events leading up to the shooting that night. He indicated he was angry about the direction his career was taking. He had to go back into the Superman series, which he did not really want to do. He did not want to act in the series but only wanted the benefits and experience of directing. He was frustrated by visitors to his home late that night. He had been suffering from a severe headache—the result of his recent head injury from a car accident.

I felt the experience unfold and watched the drama as George took total control of my body. George had awakened when two visitors, Carol von Ronkle and William Bliss, arrived at his home late that night. George yelled down to Leonore that he wasn't feeling well and to get rid of the visitors. When he heard they hadn't left, he put on his robe, went downstairs and confronted them. He spoke angrily, telling the visitors to leave because there was no party. After being chided by

Leonore about his actions, he apologized, had another drink and went back upstairs.

I could feel the throbbing pain in his right temple. I felt his anger and disgust. He sat down on the bed, took off his robe and was about to lie down when he decided to play The Game. He removed a Lugar from his bureau drawer.

At this point, Gary asked what George was feeling and George told him. I was having the same feelings also.

Shortly thereafter, George put the Lugar to his right temple and there was a searing pain in my right wrist then he lowered the gun. Taking his left hand to support his right wrist he turned the Lugar upside down with the handle pointing toward the ceiling; then he pulled the trigger.

There was a simultaneous feeling of pain in my right temple and my hand flew outward from my body. I was propelled backwards into the couch feeling George's anguish and shock. He let out a low moan, not quite a cry or a scream.

Suddenly I became aware we were looking down on George's lifeless body. Blood had started to flow from his head, mouth and nose, and there was blood and tissue splattered on the headboard of the bed. He kept moaning he didn't mean to die and it wasn't supposed to happen. After a moment, he was talking to his spirit guide, White Eagle, who told George he was dead. There was an obvious point of remembrance and George then asked White Eagle where I was. It was shortly thereafter he found me and pledged never to leave me again. I told him I would never forget what happened that night and I haven't.

After bringing us back to the present, Gary and George discussed the purpose of the reenactment, which was to reveal that George did not commit suicide. Also, George wanted Gary to believe he was an actual part of me.

Then George spoke about life choices regarding not only his death but also death in general. He indicated our paths in this lifetime were somewhat set but there were always choice variables. Those choices determined the length of time it would take to complete karmic work. Following our death, we can review the maturation and completion of our reincarnation cycle.

This experience had lasted almost two hours and we all were getting weary. Gary said he was going straight home and then to bed. Matt and I decided to go to breakfast and then home. Before we parted,

Matt said he would install a modem in Gary's computer so we could exchange information, which would make the book project easier.

Leaving the office building, Matt and I remarked on how close our old house was to Gary's office. I guess things were not in place when I lived there for this experience to happen. George said it had to happen at this time and in this way. Gary and I felt our paths must have crossed numerous times in this neighborhood, at the university, and the hospital where we both had worked. But we never really met until that class in September.

I felt we were a bit shocked at what had just transpired. Inside I could tell the day was not finished as far as the events of June 16, 1959. It had only begun!

Pages from Jean's diary describing her experience on the 37th anniversary of George Reeves' death.

6/16 Things basically went off. B5 a hitch. G. woke me up @ 2AM holding me tight weeping saying he is sorry to have to put me through this. He loves me so much. Doesn't really want me to see it all. Matt OK. Told him he could watch or not as he wanted. G. came out right away. Gary didn't need to do anything; just prompted on where he was + what was going on. Spent time on why the fake shooting they @ all. Started during service time. Went through his anger, frustration + physical pains of evening. Surprise @ actual death. Actually pulled the trigger @ the same time it happened 37 years ago. I saw the house, people + G.'s body after the shot. He really

didn't mean to die. He spoke
c̄ a spirit guide + then came
after me. Pledged to stay with
me + I said I would never
forget, and I haven't. He was
surprised I was so young. Gary
talked c̄ D about the spirit
aspect and how this final meet
came about. Why it took so long
Paths are somewhat set, but there
are close variables
Time lasted well over 1 hr close
to 2 hrs by the time we all left
We still marvel at the close
proximity of our Beta house to
his office (Gary's) and how often
our paths must have crossed
Both in the neighborhood + @ U.
+ hospitals Things never really
fell in place until 9/95 when I
started the Classes
Matt will put in a modem
for Gary as soon as Gary's room
is ready. Our computer came
today, so when Matt gets it
installed, the routing will begin
★ I very affectionate + emotional
all day. Events keep happening

The Reenactment

From the unreal, lead me to the real.
From the darkness, lead me to light.
From death, lead me to immortality.
—Brihad-Aranyaka Upanishad

TΣM

Gary

I had set aside Jean's request to meet her at my office on the anniversary of George's death so I could continue evaluating her mental status. I felt she was experiencing Dissociative Identity Disorder, and perhaps delusional, but did not have enough information to make a sound clinical judgment. I believed Jean's Dissociative Identity Disorder and delusions resulted from her attempt to cope with the accumulated tragedies she experienced as a young child.

To deal with these early tragedies, Jean began taking refuge into her fantasy world with her fantasy hero George Reeves. Over time, she infused a great amount of psychic energy into this hero fantasy figure and eventually he took on a life of his own. Once this occurred, this fantasy figure became a separate autonomous part of Jean's personality.

Although the George Reeves fantasy figure became an autonomous identity within Jean's personality structure, he still remained separated from her conscious awareness. She could feel his presence but could not communicate with him directly. Moreover, it wasn't until Jean began practicing mindfulness meditation that the psychological barriers between her autonomous self and the George Reeves fantasy figure became permeable. Once this occurred, the George Reeves identity began communicating with Jean and shortly thereafter emerged as her alter personality.

As I was gaining some insights into how the George Reeves alter personality was created, Jean kept insisting I needed to come to my office on June 16th. Jean and George both stressed that something big was going to happen on that date and I needed to be there. Feeling somewhat uncomfortable about their request, I told them again I would think about it.

Then Jean informed me she had been very depressed for over a month and disclosed this always occurs on the anniversary of George Reeves' death. She said the depressions first occurred at the age of thirteen and have continued ever since, beginning in April and lasting until mid-summer. She also indicated her son Matthew knew about the depressions and during those periods would try to lift her spirits.

Jean said the depression often became unbearable. Then George emerged and explained that Jean's depressions were so severe because his depression added to hers. He indicated that because they were twin souls, Jean always experienced what he experienced especially around the anniversary of his death.

George continued to explain that Jean's depressions coupled with his sent her on a downward spiral.

George then shifted his focus away from Jean's depressions to his death experience. He said as soon as he pulled the trigger and killed himself there was blackness, and then he felt being pulled toward a bright light. He then realized a part of him was missing and he desired to reconnect with it. Waiting for George as he moved toward the light was his spirit guide, White Eagle, and George asked White Eagle to find the missing part of his soul. White Eagle directed George to Jean. Since then Jean has had a profound awareness of George.

Jean knew many details about George Reeves' life. She knew he had not committed suicide but could not understand how she knew it. She also felt his presence and at times felt he was guiding her, but could not grasp where she was being led.

Listening to Jean and George talk about their shared depressions and the death experience, I became curious what other relevant details about their relationship they were not sharing with me. With my curiosity up, I wondered what was going to happen in my office on the anniversary date of George Reeves' death, so I finally made a decision to meet Jean in my office on Sunday June 16th.

Jean informed me George Reeves died at 1:58 a.m. Pacific time, which would make it 4:58 a.m. Eastern time. She also informed me her son Matthew would accompany her. I was glad there would be a witness to whatever was going to happen.

TΣM

On Saturday June 15, Daryl, my life-partner, set the clock for 3 a.m. We settled in for the night and I quickly fell asleep.

I awoke with a startle at 3:20 a.m. I got up, walked into the living room, sat on the couch and tried to figure out why I had awakened so abruptly. Then I realized I had to meet Jean and her son at the office.

I went back into the bedroom and looked at the clock a second time. I checked the alarm and discovered Daryl had set the clock for 3 p.m. instead of 3 a.m. How odd it was I had awakened without the alarm going off.

On the way to the office I stopped at a White Castle restaurant, got a cup of coffee and a breakfast sandwich. I arrived at the office building still wondering why I had awakened so automatically. I meandered to the office, turned on the lights and entered the consulting room. I got the tape recorder ready, prepared my coffee, sat down and relaxed.

Jean and Matthew arrived shortly after 4 a.m. After our greetings, Jean sat down on the couch and Matthew stood in the open doorway to the consulting room. After Jean was settled and comfortable, I turned on the tape recorder and shortly thereafter, she began talking about the events that happened thirty-seven years ago.

There was an abrupt shift in her consciousness and her bodily movements became less fluid. Her eyes closed as she moved into a trance and her facial expression became somber. Then her facial expression took on a harsh persona as her bodily movements became somewhat masculine, and the George Reeves alter personality emerged. Her voice changed only slightly by becoming more direct and masculine but it was still Jean's voice.

The George Reeves alter personality had taken control of Jean's body. Without warning, George began playing out a drama, which had occurred on that June night in 1959. Both Matthew and I were somewhat startled as George began talking to people as if they were in the room.

Jean got up from the sofa, her eyes tightly closed. She walked around the room talking to what appeared to be four other people. She turned back toward the sofa, walked over to it, stopped, turned to the right and started talking to whom I later learned was Leonore Lemon. George Reeves had a relationship with Lenore and was living with her at the time of his death.

George through Jean was telling Leonore there was no party that night because he had a splitting headache and needed to get some sleep. George turned away from Leonore, stopped, turned back and told her he needed rest because of the upcoming boxing match. He then turned toward the guests, told them there was no party and that they needed to leave the house immediately.

Jean then turned and it appeared by her movements she was walking up stairs and then turned again as if entering a room. She walked back over to the sofa and sat down without any attempt to put her hand on the arm of the sofa. She gently pressed her palms on the cushion and eased her body down as if sitting on a bed. She sat still for several seconds without making a sound. She then reached across the arm of the sofa to where the end table sat, opened an imaginary drawer and took out an object.

Jean made movements indicating the object was a gun. She appeared to play with the gun for a few minutes by tossing it from one hand to the other. She inspected it and rubbed it with her hands. After a long sigh, she started to bring the gun up toward her head.

I later learned that during World War II George Reeves played a game with an unloaded revolver, or Lugar. To reduce anxiety he would take an unloaded gun, point it to his head, and pull the trigger. This reckless game somehow calmed him down. After he was out of the military, he continued playing the game until the day he was killed. Many of his close friends and acquaintances knew about the game.

As Jean was bringing the imaginary gun up toward her head, she stopped in mid-action and flinched as if her right arm was in pain. She then quickly put the imaginary gun down on her lap. I later learned just before the death of the actor George Reeves, he had been in an auto accident after someone cut his car's brake lines, resulting in an injury to his head and right wrist.

Jean sat for a few seconds, then took her left hand, placed it on her right wrist and pulled her right hand with the imaginary gun up to her right temple. Using her left hand as a brace, she flipped the gun with the handle pointing up. I later learned the gun George Reeves used the night he killed himself was a German Lugar.

Stabilizing the imaginary Lugar with her left hand, Jean pulled the trigger. After the trigger was pulled, an expression of surprise spread across her face. I later discovered the actor George Reeves was unaware someone had put live ammunition in the Lugar.

When Jean pulled the imaginary trigger, both Matthew and I looked at the clock and it was 4:57 a.m. It would have been 1:57 a.m. Los Angeles time and the actor George Reeves supposedly died at 1:58 a.m., only a minute difference. It was evident by the look on Matthew's face that he was as surprised as I was, that Jean had reenacted George Reeves' death scene so close to the actual time. We were also surprised Jean acted out the entire drama with her eyes closed.

After a long silence, George began speaking through Jean about what had just occurred. Then George began to fade into the background as Jean came out of the trance.

Once I was sure Jean was okay, we decided to end the meeting and leave the office. I decided to wait until later in the day before I wrote my case notes because I was exhausted. I went home, briefly reflected on what had happened and went to bed. My sleep was very restless with fragmented dreams.

I awoke later in the afternoon, wrote my clinical notes and spent the rest of the day puzzling over the experience. I wondered how Jean could have constructed such an elaborate delusion around the actor George Reeves. Moreover, how was she able to time her reenactment of George Reeves' death so precisely? Where was Jean's awareness after the alter personality took control and reenacted George Reeves death? I wondered what she and Matthew discussed on their way home and how she would describe the experience in her diary.

TΣM

I was still puzzling over Jean's reenactment when Monday arrived. I was convinced she had read a biography on the late actor to know the intricate details about the night of his death. As I reviewed my case notes, I had many questions concerning Jean and her relationship with the alter personality.

Two o'clock that afternoon Jean and I began processing the events that had taken place in my office the day before. She indicated she was feeling okay but was a little shaken and saddened over what she had learned about George's death. George emerged and indicated he was also saddened by the choices he had made in his life, which eventually led to his murder.

As George spoke, Jean looked sad as her eyes welled up and tears began to roll down her cheeks. I could tell by the way she was acting that she was experiencing George's emotions. It was apparent there were no psychological barriers between Jean's personality and the George Reeves alter personality, which was further evidence these two identities could experience each other's feelings and emotions.

Since George was in the mood to talk, I allowed him to continue. I felt his disclosures could provide clues about how Jean had used details from a George Reeves' biography to construct her delusions. Moreover, information might surface about how Jean had constructed the George Reeves' death scene so precisely.

I asked George who were the people he was talking with at his home that night. Jean's eyes shifted to the upper left, then back to me as George began to speak. He explained that Leonore had turned on the porch light that night, which was a signal to their friends there was a party going on. A neighbor, Carol von Ronkle and an acquaintance Bill Bliss saw the light on and came by thinking there was a party, and Leonore invited them in.

George then confronted Leonore for inviting Carol and Bill into the house because there was no party. George told Carol and Bill to leave immediately and Leonore told them to stay. While George and Leonore were arguing Robert Condon, their houseguest was observing the scene. Robert Condon was a publicist covering an up coming fight between George and Archie Moore.

George indicated he had been drinking heavily that day and had a splitting headache. After the altercation, he went up stairs to the bedroom, took off his robe, sat on the bed and played the game with his Lugar. As soon as he put the Lugar to his head and pulled the trigger, he knew what had happened and who was responsible. Toni and Eddie Mannix had him murdered. George said his ex-lover Toni Mannix was insanely jealous of other women, especially Leonore Lemon whom was much younger.

George reiterated experiencing the blackness, being pulled toward a bright light, meeting White Eagle, and finding Jean.

George said there were several clues about his impending doom. There were three attempts on his life during the weeks leading up to his death. The first occurred when he was driving in the Hollywood area and two trucks pulled into his lane. One truck was in front of him and the other behind, sandwiching him. The trucks kept getting closer and closer until one tapped his rear bumper. He thought at the time this was just a scare tactic from Toni.

The second incident occurred when George was walking down Wilshire Boulevard in Los Angeles when an unknown car tried to run him down on the sidewalk.

Third, someone cut the brake lines on his car. This caused an accident, which resulted in an injury to his head and right wrist.

George then revealed that on several occasions after his death he visited the Benedict Canyon house, the scene of his murder. He also visited Toni in her home and indicated she spent the remainder of her life watching his old Superman TV movies. She remained depressed and became a recluse. He also visited his mother Helen who was depressed and in denial over his death. She too ended up becoming a recluse. One way Helen coped with George's death was to build a shrine to him composed of his pictures and memorabilia.

I asked George had he ever haunted the Benedict Canyon house. Jean smiled and George indicated he had never remained in the house long enough to haunt it. George further explained that when Toni Mannix died her soul remained earth bound because she was so possessive of her earthly treasures. Because she was earth bound, she would visit the Benedict Canyon house searching for George.

George explained Toni had given him the down payment for the Benedict Canyon house. Because Toni was so possessive, she felt she owned the house and George along with it. Although he had split up with Toni, everything he owned including the house was willed to her.

After Toni died, her spirit went directly to the house hoping George would meet her there. He did meet her at the house on several occasions and even as a spirit, she wanted him back as her lover. He informed Toni that would be impossible because he had connected with the other part of his soul.

I found these details interesting, but had no idea whether they were accurate. I continued wondering if Jean had read a biography on the actor and had confabulated the story, creating a delusion, and projecting those details into her alter personality. I wondered how Toni Mannix fit into Jean's delusional system. My hunch was Toni was the shadow side of Jean's personality.

What was perplexing about the alter personality's story was his continuing reference that he was a spirit. I felt this was how Jean legitimized him.

Realigning Of The Spirits

*When you make the two one
and when you make the inside like the outside
and the outside like the inside
and the above like the below...*
—The Gospel of Thomas (saying 22)

Sunday June 16, 1996

After leaving Gary's office, Matt and I went to a restaurant for breakfast as planned. While eating, my emotions were waxing and waning over the morning's events. In the background, I could hear George talking about his agent, Art Weissman, as well as the police informing Helen about his death. As George spoke I felt an overwhelming desire to cry. Matt noticed the tears welling up in my eyes and asked what was wrong. Rather than allowing me to answer, he quickly joked about the quality of the food. I assured him it wasn't the food. He didn't ask any more questions and we remained silent throughout the rest of the meal.

The eerie silence persisted on the way home as I continued dealing with the influx of thoughts and feelings coming from George. Once home, Matt went straight to bed and, since Duncan wasn't up yet, the house was quiet. I sat alone in the living room listening to George reliving the drama that occurred in the Benedict Canyon house that night.

George described the police arriving and, shortly thereafter, the men from the coroner's office. Several officials chuckled and sarcastically remarked that since George was Superman, the man of steel, why couldn't he save himself? While this bantering was going on, another young official was on the verge of nausea because of the blood and tissue that had been splattered about the room.

I could feel George's anger over the "man of steel" remark and surmised he would have thrown the men out of the house if he could have. As George talked, I could tell by the tone of his voice there was much confusion in the house that night. I could hear voices of men and women all talking at once. To gain some semblance of order, two officers took the occupants of the house into separate rooms to be questioned.

I heard Duncan walk out of the bedroom. He asked how things went at the meeting with Gary.

I said, "Things went okay."

Without another word spoken, Duncan and I sat in the early morning silence reading the newspaper. I felt exhausted. I walked out of the living room without saying a word and went to bed.

Later in the afternoon, Duncan, Matt, and I went shopping for a computer so I could get started writing the book. This helped divert my attention away from George, but I was still aware he was reliving the events leading up to the night of his death.

By evening, George seemed somewhat settled as if he had come to terms with the events of the day. In bed, I could feel him curled up around me in a protective position. I asked how was he feeling and he said fine and then commented he was glad the day was over. I was also glad because of the continual emotional mood swings I felt from George throughout the day. As I drifted off to sleep, I found myself reliving the events of the day all over again.

I awoke with a startle and looked at the clock. It was the time of George's death. I wondered if we would be reliving this hour forever.

Monday June 17, 1996

The meeting with Gary was very intense because it was a rehash of Sunday's drama. I remarked how I could feel George's emotions throughout the entire day and Gary commented he thought that might happen. After discussing my feelings, Gary then shifted the focus to George. He could not understand why George had left his entire estate to Toni Mannix. George explained he and Toni had made a prior agreement regarding his estate and the agreement was not changed or altered after their relationship ended.

After discussing George's agreement with Toni, Gary then inquired why George came to me after his death. Again, George explained that we are two parts of the same soul. He continued to reiterate that we are special because of our twin soul bond and there are not many couples bonded the way we are.

As George finished explaining our twin soul connection, Gary commented that he had a feeling George made contact with him Sunday morning. Gary sensed it was George who woke him up so he wouldn't be late for our meeting. George admitted he did make contact because he knew the clock settings were wrong. George said he nudged Gary out of a deep sleep so the day would go off as scheduled. It appears George has broken through Gary's protective barriers, which means they can now connect psychically.

Everything was going fine until I made an impulsive gesture and discovered George's temper. I was so appreciative that Gary came to his office for the meeting that when he gave me the customary post-session hug, I gave him a quick kiss on the cheek. George then became a bit crazy and I could feel his anger like a bomb going off.

I quickly left Gary's office and discovered I had forgotten my water bottle so I returned for it. I informed Gary, George was very angry over the kiss. Gary said I should be careful about my boundaries to which George or possibly I, replied, "Some things don't change even after death!"

After finally leaving Gary's office, I drove to Columbus to spend a few days with Matthew. George talked the entire way about the kiss. I now know that the gratitude I gave to Gary was at the wrong time and was the wrong thing to do. The kiss occurred in such a short time after the events of Sunday morning that George felt vulnerable.

I felt George's anger was a bit melodramatic but a good demonstration he still has a well-rounded set of emotions. I can now understand what Jack Larson meant when being interviewed about George. Jack said George's anger on the Superman set was at times volcanic. I love George too much and have waited too long to jeopardize our relationship. I surely don't want to face this type of situation again.

Tuesday June 18, 1996

After a restful night's sleep, I decided to go to a strawberry farm near Matt's apartment and pick strawberries to make jam. I haven't picked strawberries since we moved from our Indiana home a few years ago. On the way to the farm, George sang love songs and was contrite for losing his temper with me yesterday.

He tried to please me more than usual by being very loving. I vowed I would never do anything again to make him angry with me even though the incident with Gary was very innocent. I also find making up with George is just as good as with a flesh and blood man.

After an enjoyable day with Matt, I settled in for the night. I had the recurring dream of my fatal car accident again. In the dream the accident was very vivid, although it happened quickly. My neck was broken and I died instantly but the medical authorities were puzzled because it appeared I should not have died.

Shortly after I died in the dream, George was there waiting and immediately took me to Coltran. It was a beautiful sunny day and we walked hand-in-hand near the water's edge. I could feel the warmth of the sand as it cushioned my every step. As we playfully waded in the warm, aqua surf, I felt George's eyes embrace me.

He told me he wanted to get back to our home as he gently put his arm around my waist. He guided me up to our bedroom and I found myself gazing into his dancing blue eyes. He smiled that wonderful George Reeves smile and I kissed the ridge of the cleft of his chin. There was no mistake about who he is. He hasn't changed. I guess we don't change much throughout our many incarnations.

Wednesday June 19, 1996

I woke up early and after having a brief conversation with Matt, I headed back to Cincinnati. George appeared to be happy. Intermittently throughout the drive, he sang oldies songs in concert with the radio. When a song came on he didn't recognize, we talked business. He insisted we get started on the book, particularly putting the outline in order.

When the conversation lulled, I reflected on Matt and how I always have a good time when we're together. I also thought about Matt's apartment. For a first home, I found it to be warm, comfortable and well organized. Of course, I would see it that way because I am his proud Mom.

Upon arriving back home, I felt tension when I was around Duncan and then realized it was coming from George. George doesn't like Duncan and doesn't like him being around. George has told me he wants me back totally. I know if things get crazy between Duncan and me, I could live with Matt for awhile because he has plenty of room.

Later at work, I was confronted with the possibility that my hours could be cut. The grandmother of the child I've been working with said the agency called and indicated the funds for the case were running out. George told me not to worry because he would take care of the situation the way he has before.

Thursday June 20, 1996

I have been aware of George's presence all day long because it feels like I'm wearing a coat when he's around. He persuaded me to watch one of the Superman tapes I have in my collection. I normally don't watch them because George isn't proud of the work he did in the series. He does like the older episodes better and I must agree that the acting, scripts, and even the sets appear to have been given more thought. The later episodes appear to have been rushed through an assembly line and George indicated they were always in a hurry.

Later in the day, Gary informed me he wants to have a book meeting. With Gary's interest, I am now motivated to go to the library and start gathering background information on George's life. Although I have a lot of material, there are many gaps because my earlier focus was mainly on the Superman character.

The information I'm looking for has to do with George's Cincinnati connection and his childhood in Illinois and Kentucky. This will give me a perspective on what George's life was like before he went into show business. I think this information will be hard to find because there has been so little written about his personal life.

Monday June 24, 1996

Finally, Matt came for a visit and put my computer together. Now that the major obstacle to writing has been cleared, I spent the remainder of the morning in the library before seeing Gary. As I was looking for information on Galesburg, Illinois where George spent his early childhood, I realized how much I enjoyed research.

In my research, I discovered Eleanor Needles, George's former wife was from Cincinnati. She now lives in Los Angeles and no longer has a Cincinnati connection because most of her family and friends in the area have long since died. I reasoned based on George's age, she would most likely be in her late seventies by now and probably does not wish to rehash old wounds. So, in lieu of getting information from Eleanor, I decided to write Jim Beaver who was George's biographer and has appeared in several TV documentaries.

Later during session, I noticed a shift in Gary's therapeutic focus. He spent most of the time questioning George and I have been noticing Gary doing that more frequently. They talked about the development of their past-life friendship in the years preceding the Civil War.

Gary then brought up the subject of his intense dislike for the man George Reeves and wondered how that dislike originated. George said it had to do with their relationship with me as Suzanne MacIntosh in that lifetime.

George explained that his name was John Stevens and Gary's was Robert Allen and they were best friends, almost like brothers. However, their friendship went sour shortly after John and I married. John discovered Robert desired to have a three-way relationship with John and me. John couldn't suppress his jealousy and anger and started a fight with Robert. He gave Robert a concussion that left him blind in one eye, broke his left arm, and left the side of his face a bloody mess.

Robert was a husky man, capable of defending himself, but he allowed John to beat him nearly to death. Although Robert lived through the ordeal, John spent the remainder of his life in repentance and restitution.

Gary wanted to know what could be done to undo the negative karma between him and George. It was apparent the negative feelings Gary had toward George surfaced in his dislike for him in the Superman series. George indicated he would do anything to undo the karmic debt but Gary also had to forgive George for what happened so long ago.

This incident is preventing George from connecting with Gary psychically. Although George did poke through Gary's protective barrier on June 16th to wake him up, that has yet to be repeated.

George thinks that if I could achieve an alpha state—a state with fewer barriers—in Gary's office, that he might make a psychic connection with Gary. The protective barrier is more intense at Gary's home.

Thursday June 27, 1996

Agency work can be worrisome if all your cases are in the hospital at the same time. But after much worry, the extra hours for my primary case came through as George promised. I feel at peace knowing I will never need to worry about work again because George will always provide.

Later, George had me watch one of his old movies, Lydia, and it appeared he enjoyed working with this particular crew. In the movie, George's character begins as a younger man and over time grows older. George wanted me to see this character so I would get an idea of what he would have looked like as an older man.

Sunday June 30, 1996

George woke me up at four fifty eight in the morning the same time he shot himself. I could feel the experience with him was very intense and could feel his emotional pain. Suddenly I was at the point of ecstasy and felt as if I were levitating. Then I felt a status orgasm, if there is such a thing, in which I was not in the here and now, but joined with him just floating somewhere in the cosmos. I don't know how long it lasted but I was conscious of being back in my bed after a few moments and soon entered a vivid dreamy sleep.

Wednesday July 3, 1996

George woke me up early and suggested we go to Sharon Woods for a relaxing walk. The path we usually take was like a green-canopied cathedral and arching over the pathway were old oak and maple trees blocking out the sun. No one else was on the path so I leaned against a stately oak tree and felt its energy vibrating throughout my body and engulf me in peace. Nearby, a smaller tree was giving off seedpods, shimmering yellow in the sun's rays penetrating the lush canopy.

In perfect bliss, I walked to a small lake, bought an ice cream cone from a park vendor, and sat watching the ducks and geese begging for morsels of food from boaters. A few ducks had waddled up on the bank and were sunning and preening their feathers. George and I walked across a road and down some cement steps to a waterfall formed by the lake's runoff. I sat on a containment wall near the walkway to take in the beauty.

I meditated as I watched the meandering stream. The sun sparkled in the water with the prismatic colors. A hummingbird sipped nectar from a purple flower, and a long necked turtle came out of the water to sun itself.

As I sat meditating, George talked about our beautiful home in Coltran. Suddenly I became aware of another voice deep inside. It was a small quiet voice telling me that George, Gary, and I were heading in the right direction and to continue on that path with faith. Then the most peaceful feeling I have ever experienced moved throughout my being.

I was brought out of my reverie upon hearing voices on the steps behind me. My alone time with George was over. To keep the peaceful feeling going, I retraced my steps along the pathway and had a feeling of oneness with this new voice, which I've decided to call the "Old One."

Twin Souls Merging

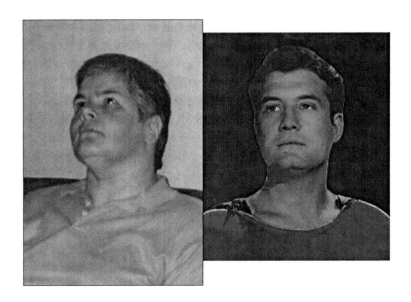

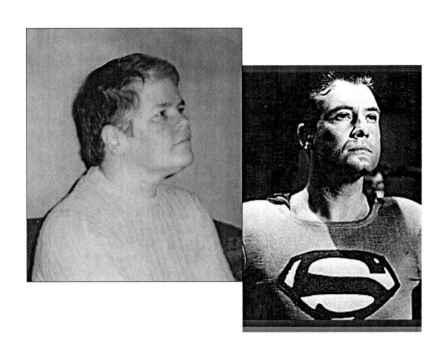

A Psychological & Spiritual Journey

This photo series shows Jean Cline at various therapeutic stages after Gary began noticing in her the image and likeness of George Reeves. She is compared here with various photos found on the Internet.

Unexpected Client

I sent my Soul through the Invisible,
Some letter of that After-life to spell,
And, by and by my Soul returned to me,
An answer "I myself am Heav'n and Hell."
    —Omar Khayyam

TΣM

Gary

After several days of intense mood swings, George finally disclosed to Jean that when she reenacted the night of his death and innocently kissed me on the cheek some unresolved issues from his past came bubbling to the surface. He indicated he was having difficulty resolving the issues by himself and felt he needed my assistance. He asked Jean if it would be okay if she allowed him to work on those issues during her therapy sessions. He stressed the issues he needed to resolve concerned the poor choices he made in his life, especially choices with women. He also emphasized these issues were creating problems in the relationship between him and Jean.

I informed Jean if I worked with George, I would have to put her issues on hold for awhile because it would probably take several sessions to help him work through his issues. She indicated that would be okay because in the last few sessions I have mainly talked with George anyway. I felt working with George would be an excellent opportunity to penetrate deeper into Jean's unconscious, in the hope of gathering more details on how she created the George Reeves alter personality.

Jean then told me that ever since she reenacted the night of George's death she could feel his emotions fluctuating between elation, anxiety, and depression. Over the weekend while watching a video of *Unsolved Mysteries* about George's death, she could feel his strong emotions as the narrator described each scene. She pointed out while watching the program there were moments when she could feel a profound sadness and George would explain what had been happening in his life during that time.

I asked George what the situations were in the *Unsolved Mysteries* tape that triggered such strong emotions. He said that although the program did not specifically focus on his mother, Helen, it did bring up bad memories about their relationship. He said his mother was a very controlling woman and throughout his life he felt trapped in a world she had created for him. Helen regulated and controlled every aspect of his life, even making decisions for him. She told him whom to play with, whom to associate with, even whom to date.

Because of his mother's wealth George said he had everything he wanted materially, but this did not make up for not having a father. During lonely moments, he would ask about his father and Helen was always evasive. She would tell him his father died when he was a baby and then change the subject. She told him he was good looking, better than the others, and someday would be a big movie star.

Helen's intense obsession for George to become a movie star prompted her to contact her half-sister who lived in Los Angeles to get a sense of what the Hollywood community was like. Shortly thereafter Helen moved George from Galesburg, Illinois to Pasadena, California.

Helen soon met and married Frank Bessolo, a banker whose family was in the wine business. Frank was the first positive male role model in George's life. George said the years he had with Frank were the happiest in his childhood. Frank became the only father George ever knew and he loved Frank deeply. Frank treated George as his own son, creating a paternal bond in which George felt secure, comfortable, and loved.

As George talked about Frank, I noticed a sudden shift in his emotions. At that point, Jean's facial expressions saddened as tears began streaming down her cheeks. She quickly explained she could feel George's deep emotional sorrow over Frank and it was overwhelming. Then her facial expressions became less intense as George remembered a trip he and Frank took to the California wine country. He remarked that those were the good times; ones he'd never forget.

Helen was insanely jealous of George's relationship with Frank. Helen felt she was losing control over George's life because of Frank's influence. She filed for divorce and prohibited Frank from ever seeing George again. George was devastated.

As George was weaving a most interesting story about his life, I was trying to integrate the details into an overall picture I had of Jean's life. It appeared on the surface Jean and George had lived very different lives. Although different, I assumed George's traits were a part of Jean's personality that she had projected onto the George Reeves image.

The details Jean projected onto George could possibly represent some traits from the shadow side of her personality. I believed these traits symbolized fragments of Jean's personality she unconsciously would not own because the traits did not fit into the overall picture of whom she perceived herself to be. Simultaneously, George emerged as Jean's hero archetype, which took on the dimensions of her friend, lover, and rescuer.

As George continued discussing the relationship he had with his mother, it became apparent there was a lack of strong ego boundaries between the two, which was similar to the relationship Jean had with her mother. Although, Jean's relationship with her mother appeared positive, George's relationship with his mother was negative. It was apparent Jean had projected the negative attributes she had toward her father onto the relationship George had with his mother.

Because of Jean's poor bonding with her father and the abrupt death of her mother, she had poor relationships with people in general, especially with men. The men Jean chose were cold, distant, controlling, and emotionally absent, just like her father.

Jean's relationship with her father was projected onto the George Reeves alter personality. George said that his mother was very controlling, as were the other women in his life. He said that the women he chose were carbon copies of his mother.

Throughout George's life, he continued to bond with women who were controlling and dominating, which eventually led to a dysfunctional relationship with Toni Mannix. George first met Toni while he was married to Eleanor Needles. Before discussing his relationship with Toni Mannix, George first needed to tell me about an incident that happened in New York. While living in New York with Eleanor, his mother was constantly interfering in their marriage.

During this time, George had many auditions and finally landed a part in a play. One day after rehearsal, an old man named Don Brewer approached him backstage and told George he was his father. George told the man he must be mistaken because his name was George Bessolo and his father was dead. The old man smiled, took out an old ragged piece of paper from his coat pocket and showed it to George. The paper was a birth certificate bearing the name George Keefer Brewer, his mother Helen's name, and the name Don Brewer.

Helen had located Don Brewer in a town near the Galesburg, Illinois and paid him to go to New York to tell George he was his father. George also discovered he was conceived out of wedlock and shortly after his birth Helen paid Don Brewer to get out of her life.

Helen was trying to create more conflicts in George's marriage, but the incident backfired on her. After that day, George refused to have anything to do with her for several years. Helen's constant meddling put a major strain on George's marriage, which eventually led to him and Eleanor having extramarital affairs. The infidelity led to divorce.

The information George disclosed about his life did not fit with the information I had about Jean's life. I believed these details regarding the actor's life were projected onto George from the shadow side of Jean's personality. Jean not only created the alter personality, but an entire life history to go with it.

TΣM

In the next meeting, Jean indicated George had been very restless after talking about his life. His emotions ran the gamut from anger to sorrow and all the emotions in between.

Although George was feeling emotionally raw, he wasted no time disclosing more details about his relationship with his mother. He stressed she became the primary instrument in creating situations that ultimately screwed up his life. Helen used her wealth to manipulate men. She made wimps of them all, except for Frank. Frank would always stand his ground because he too was from wealth and had a strong personality. When Helen discovered she could not control Frank, she divorced him. The divorce was her way of controlling the situation.

George angrily admitted that he allowed Helen to control him with her money. He felt like a wimp. He became wimpy with other women as well. Once George was able to disclose this, he began letting go of some of the anger toward himself and toward his mother.

After his anger subsided, I helped George reframe his life. I helped him understand that those bad situations helped him become more aware of himself and by being more aware, he was a stronger person. I suspected what George was expressing about his mother was in reality what Jean felt about her father. I believed by helping George, I was helping Jean get in touch with her emotions and parts of herself she had disowned. I was helping her reclaim those attributes, which she had split off from herself and projected onto George.

George became anxious when the topic turned to Toni Mannix. Once again, he started questioning his manhood. He sadly admitted a stupid deal he made to get ahead in the movie industry.

While still married to Eleanor, George was at a Hollywood party mingling with the crowd, prospecting for acting jobs. At that party, he met Eddie and Toni Mannix. Toni was a beautiful woman and her husband Eddie was a very influential Hollywood executive. George noticed Toni appeared to be interested in him but the situation did not allow them to interact much.

Several years later, after George and Eleanor divorced he attended another Hollywood party. George had been in the Army and out of the Hollywood scene for a while. He was having trouble getting acting jobs. At the party, he was hoping to meet someone who could help him kick-start his acting career when he met Eddie Mannix a second time.

Eddie cornered George and indicated he could arrange for George to obtain good acting roles. Eddie took George's arm and led him into an adjacent room where they could talk privately.

Eddie offered George a deal he could not resist. The deal was if George would take care of Eddie's wife, Toni, then Eddie would take care of George's career. At first George did not understand what Eddie meant by "taking care" of his wife. Eddie then claimed that, because of his failing health and the heart medication he took, he was impotent and could no longer satisfy Toni's voracious sexual appetite.

Despite Eddie's claim of impotence, George later discovered he was having an affair with another woman.

Eddie informed George that Toni had been interested in him from the first moment she laid eyes on him and wanted George to be her lover. George felt this offer was too good to be true and figured a few nights in the hay would satisfy her. He would get the movie parts he wanted and get on with his career. George made the deal with Eddie, but the only major role he landed was being Toni's lover. She, like Helen, controlled his life.

George eventually fell in love with Toni but as he aged, he began to question his feelings for her. Toni loved the fast lane, but the years of partying were taking their toll on her. Her looks were fading fast. Toni was seven years George's senior. This combined with her fading beauty caused her to become insecure. She became even more controlling, possessive, and demanding.

Toni became a black widow wanting to consume him. When she wanted something, she went after it and would not stop until she got it. And once she had it, she wouldn't let go.

George said he continued to stay with Toni after Eddie reneged on the bargain because he fell in love with her. Her unreasonable demands, however, began to push George away. Like Helen, she began telling him whom he could befriend and how to live his life.

It was obvious Toni and George had a codependent relationship. Even after their break up, Toni still paid George's bills. They just couldn't let go of each other. As codependents, they created a mutually destructive bond and a subconscious agreement to sabotage their relationship. They unconsciously sustained pathological behaviors in their relationship.

I had a sense Jean had projected her codependent patterns onto the fantasy character of George Reeves. It appeared Jean had done this as a way of disowning the unhealthy situations she found herself in. I felt George was a refuge, which enabled Jean to escape ego-threatening situations.

The Hollywood atmosphere dominated George creating a false sense of self. The Hollywood experience took away his identity and left him feeling shallow and empty. He became what Hollywood wanted him to be just as Jean became what her father wanted her to be. George was caught in the Hollywood fantasy web as Jean was caught in her father's web. George began to believe his outer persona was really who he was. Jean believed her fantasy life was really who she was. George didn't know who he was and neither did Jean. I felt George was a reflection of Jean's inner identity struggles.

TΣM

Working with the alter personality George Reeves has given me insight into the inner dynamics of Jean's personality structure. Based on this information, I am now positive Jean has created George out of a deep psychological need to cope with her numerous losses and controlling father.

In her early years, Jean had an intense symbiotic relationship with her mother, which contributed to blurred ego boundaries between the two. Jean's identity was fused with her mother's, creating a situation in which her mother was living through Jean and vice versa. Consequently, Jean did not develop a healthy core sense of self.

Symbiotic relationships are formed shortly after birth and are part of normal childhood development. These relationships usually last through the first few years of life in which the mother and child become emotionally and psychically bonded. This process gives the child a sense of safety and security and forms their identity. Normally, the mother eventually allows the child to separate and become autonomous. The child differentiates itself from its mother and develops a core sense of self.

This core sense of self did not develop appropriately in Jean because of her mother's psychological need for companionship. After her mother died, there was a deep emptiness in Jean's life. Jean tried to fill this emptiness by unsuccessfully attempting to create a positive relationship with her father. This failure to bond with her father led to frustration and anger. Jean repressed these negative feelings and attempted to transform them into positive ones. However, her anger and frustration toward her father remained unresolved. The repression of these unresolved negative feelings and attempting to transform them into positive feelings and actions eventually led to an unhealthy codependent relationship with her father and later with her brother and two husbands.

Once the codependent patterns were formed, Jean could no longer express her anger and frustration over the dysfunctional situation she found herself in. It was during this period she began to move more frequently into her fantasy world. In this fantasy world, Jean began using her imaginary playmate George Reeves as her father and rescuer.

She projected onto this fantasy character all the positive attributes that were lacking in her father. Over time, this George Reeves fantasy character split from her personality forming an alter personality. Eventually George evolved into Jean's lover, friend, and rescuer. Once formed, this alter personality and hero archetype became a separate autonomous functioning part of Jean's personality with its own separate detailed life history.

    While working with George, I gained vital insights into the dynamics of Jean's personality. On a macro level I understood how Jean created the alter personality as a coping strategy to deal with her losses and her dysfunctional family situation. On a micro level, I still did not understand how Jean processed the information on a daily basis. I felt if I had access to Jean's uncensored diary, I would possibly find the critical information needed to answer these questions.

Discovery Of What We Were

*Two souls with but a single thought,
Two hearts that beat as one.*
—von Munch-Bellinghausen

TΣM

Sunday July 7, 1996

Once again, George brought up the subject that he and I were twin souls. He explained because of our twin soul connection we have many life parallels, which have manifested in the various incarnations. He indicated there were several parallels that linked us within this lifetime ranging from our educational backgrounds to our family history. I found this new concept very exciting and also discovered that even our astrological signs were compatible.

Tuesday July 9, 1996

As I was discovering life parallels between George and me, I also found out I was connected to Gary as well. This became evident when I found out Gary had become ill over the weekend after using paint solvents and developed a headache and an upset stomach. During this same period, I too mysteriously developed a severe case of gastritis.

Once I discovered Gary was ill I wanted to lift his spirits and thought of sending him a get-well card, but then had second thoughts because Gary doesn't seem like a get-well card type person. George suggested if we could find a card with James Dean on it that would be just as good, though I was a bit skeptical.

After checking all the card shops in the mall, I came up empty, but George wanted to give it one more try. I said okay if he would take the lead. He guided me to a video store and on the back wall was a metal display rack with postcards of celebrities and to my surprise; there was one with James Dean. I was flabbergasted and to top it off, George wrote a message on the card to Gary and even signed it.

After returning home, I decided to relax and meditate. George took me back to Georgia and this time I saw more of the house we lived in, which was a one and a half story structure. A large parlor ran across the entire front of the house with fireplaces located at both ends. Near one of the fireplaces was a conversation area with a sofa, two upholstered chairs, and one straight-backed wooden chair. There was a staircase leading up to the second floor, which did not quite bisect the room.

The floor was made with wide dark pine planks with a muticolored woven rug as the centerpiece. Situated at one end of the room was a pianoforte with two wooden chairs and a bench. There were several small end tables decorated with oil lamps and candleholders. The walls appeared to be white washed with a tabby texture and the room was light and cheery.

I suddenly became aware I was viewing the house through Suzanne MacIntosh's eyes. I was reading a letter informing me that my husband John had been killed in battle and there by my side to console me was Robert Allen. My eldest son George Robert was angry over his father's death and wanted to enlist in the Georgia militia. Robert finally helped my son to calm down and pointed out he should not enlist in the military because he was needed on the plantation.

As Robert was consoling me, I got the chance to see more of what he looked like physically. He resembled Gary though somewhat huskier. It was obvious Robert spent most of his time outdoors because his complexion was tan and his hair was sandy brown and rather streaked by the sun.

Usually Robert appears clean-shaven in my meditations, but this time he was wearing a bushy mustache. The majority of men during this period grew facial hair—metal for razors was scarce due to the war effort. Robert had a scar on his left cheek from where John had hit him years before. His eyes were the same grayish-blue with gold speckles as Gary's are today.

As I was looking into Robert's eyes, I noticed I was having strong feelings toward him.

George brought me back to the present before any romantic involvement could occur. However, I already knew Robert and I had a romantic relationship that began while I was grieving over the loss of John. The grief left me physically ill and it was only through Robert's care that I survived at all.

Monday July 15, 1996

On the way to Gary's office George and I discussed our life parallels. It was odd that two genetically unrelated people almost a generation apart could have so much in common.

While I was telling Gary about the life parallels, he commented he could feel George's energy emanating from me. This prompted Gary to suggest he and George should attempt another telepathic experiment, possibly tomorrow night. If both George and Gary can feel each other's energy in the office then the experiment might be successful.

Wednesday July 17, 1996

Gary called this afternoon and indicated he thought the telepathic experiment was successful. He remarked at first he was having problems maintaining focus because of a severe headache but he eventually did feel George's energy. George confirmed they did make contact and indicated he liked Gary's meditation room and found it very esoteric. George explained further that in several of Gary's incarnations he had been interested in magic and voodoo. Even the slaves on the plantation where Gary worked shared their magical knowledge with him.

As he came out of meditation, Gary noticed the James Dean postcard I had sent with George's signature. He compared the signature with one on a publicity photo of George I had given him earlier. Gary said the signatures were very similar.

After the experiment, George indicated he was exhausted because it took more energy to break away from me as I was awake. I told George that next time he and Gary try this, it should be done while I'm asleep.

By mid-afternoon, George seemed to have recovered his depleted energy. He joked and teased as I cleaned the house. I told him I would have less to do if he would stop leaving his dust all over the place—a joke because he was cremated. He got a kick out of that.

Monday July 22, 1996

I am now very aware of George's energy presence because there is a tingling sensation around my left ear. When we are fully connected, it's like wearing a glove over my entire body. When feeling George's energy presence, the range of emotions he exhibits astounds me.

While making calls to Los Angeles, Galesburg, and Iowa regarding the book project, I suddenly became aware of George's sadness. He said that the calls were bringing back memories, good and bad. I could then feel his presence over my body and realized because of those memories he needed my affection and reassurance. It's odd that a spirit has this need.

Tuesday July 23, 1996

Today started with George in a loving mood, telling me that when we are together the angels sing and the Old Ones rejoice. Gary finally accepted the new business letterhead for the book project and everything looked rosy. Then I came across an article in the *Cincinnati Enquirer*, which stated a new book on George Reeves' life would be published in November.

I read the article three times before I fully realized what it said. It indicated the authors of the book thought Toni Mannix had killed George.

George remarked he didn't know anything about the book or the authors but felt our book would be much different.

Thursday July 25, 1996

Gary finally returned my call. He seemed encouraged by the new book on George's life. George keeps telling me our book will be different. I guess I have to take that on faith. Having faith is now difficult because Matthew again attempted to install a modem in Gary's computer, without success.

Monday July 29, 1996

Gary indicated George made psychic contact with him on Friday. While meditating, Gary felt a tingling sensation and pictured George in the Superman costume. George said that new psychic pathways had been forged, which allowed him to easily contact Gary.

I discovered three more life parallels between me and George. We were both in our chosen professions for twenty-eight years. We each grew up with the same gender parent absent from the home, and the parents who raised us both died in June.

I told Gary that I had a dream in which I saw a tombstone with the date December 12, 1996. What does it mean?

Tuesday July 30, 1996

Today, Gary and I finally had a meeting regarding the book project. I showed Gary a scrapbook, which contained a newspaper picture of Toni Mannix. Gary said Toni's photograph looked like a picture I had shown him of George's mother, Helen.

Gary said Toni and Helen also appeared to be close together in age, and perhaps that's why George hooked up with Leonore Lemon who was much younger. George said Leonore was about ten years his junior. He was in a mid-life crisis when they met and he could not accept getting older.

Gary and I decided to increase our sessions to two hours on regression days. There was lots of information surfacing and we needed more time to process is. We also decided that on the nights before the regressions, George would attempt to transfer his energy to Gary to stimulate regression imagery by allowing Gary to probe for more details.

Thursday August 5, 1996

During a psychic transfer, Gary saw George in his Civil War uniform. Since the imagery was so vivid, Gary decided to regress me again back to that period. He wanted more details regarding the last time I saw John alive.

When the regression scene opened, I saw myself as Suzanne. I was very emotional because I knew John was going off to battle and I'd never see him again. I begged him not to go as he took the last horse and his personal servant, whom he would later free. With tears in my eyes, he turned and walked away, leaving Robert Allen to manage the plantation.

This time it was strange to feel Suzanne's emotions as my own. I now know these feelings are inside of me and I have no control over them.

It was difficult coming back to waking consciousness. It was almost like the experience I had in class when I could not come out of the trance. It took Gary two times to count me back to the present. I was spacey for quite awhile after coming out.

Later, I contacted a private researcher in Galesburg, Illinois to get information on Helen's life. The research department of the Galesburg library did not look up old news articles, which I found rather odd.

Wednesday August 7, 1996

I awoke to a beautiful lovemaking experience with George, and afterwards felt a bit spacey. It seemed different from just being tired. I had not felt this before. I tried grounding myself by working on the computer but the feeling would not go away. Concerned, I called Gary. After explaining what had happened he felt that being together all the time and making love with George was zapping my energy.

Gary said he could help me create a sanctuary in my inner world where George would not be allowed to enter. I could go there and rest when I needed to. This upset George, but I felt it would be the best solution.

Thursday August 8, 1996

In session today, we explored my recent surreal emotions. Gary concluded I was being drained of energy due to my hectic work schedule and George's lovemaking demands. Gary then tried to hypnotize me but George resisted. Finally, with Gary's persuasion, George let go and I went under.

Gary guided me in creating an imaginary room George and I could retreat to. The room had an antechamber that was off limits to George. This was my private resting sanctuary and it was similar to a bedroom. We created a special area in the outer room where George could wait while I rested. The sanctuary was serene and relaxing. It was a beautiful place where I could get away for awhile.

Gary began bringing me out of the trance but George tried to keep me there. Gary got a good sense of George's will. Gary had to count me out of the trance twice before George would release his hold.

Reluctantly, George admitted to Gary that he realized he had made love to me too much yesterday. He explained that because he so enjoys giving me pleasure, he forgot I was mortal and needed rest.

It then dawned on me that, because Matthew is helping with the book, he will eventually find out about my sexual relationship with George. I don't know how well he will handle it. After discussing this with Gary, he indicated he would find a way to broach the subject with Matt and help him understand what's happening. I felt this would be the best route because Matt and Gary have developed a trusting relationship.

After leaving Gary's office, George pleaded with me not to lock him out when I go into my sanctuary. He said he had waited eighty-two years for me and could not stand the thought of our separation. I reassured him the separation was only for a short period while I rested. I hoped this would not drive George away. He assured me it wouldn't.

Sunday August 11, 1996

Once again, the modem could not be installed in Gary's computer because of software problems. This occurred when Matt mistakenly took the modem disks through a metal detector at work scrambling all the information. There seems to be problem after problem trying to install the modem and I wondered if it's because of unseen forces. Matt is very computer savvy. This simple modem installation should not be a problem.

Gary and I spoke by phone and he informed me he was feeling more of George's energy and getting vivid images during their telepathic experiments. Sometimes George is in his Civil War attire; other times in the Superman costume. I get the feeling George is joking with Gary by wearing the Superman costume because he refuses to wear it when I see him.

Later I discovered another life parallel between me and George. We are both claustrophobic. His claustrophobia formed as a small child after older playmates had locked him in a cellar. I do not know where my claustrophobia originated. Perhaps from my past-life death from consumption or from being placed in the incubator after I was born.

Wednesday August 14, 1996

I finally got in touch with the independent researcher in Galesburg, Illinois. He seemed interested in our book project and said he would charge ten dollars an hour to do the research. This sounds like a lot of money, but going there myself would be more costly. Besides, the researcher knows his way around the local library system, which means a lot when you're doing research.

I then contacted a supervisor from *Unsolved Mysteries* in the hope of getting Jack Larson's address. They could not disclose any information about Jack, but they did give me his agent's address.

George seems happy we have started on this phase of the book project and indicated there is something he needs to convey to Jack.

Monday August 19, 1996

I decided to locate Noel Neil who played the second Lois Lane in the Superman TV series. I contacted the Screen Actors Guild. They were very helpful and gave me Noel's phone number. I also inquired about Phyllis Coates who played the first Lois Lane and the Guild no longer had a listing for her.

I felt that since Noel had worked with George for so long, she could verify the information I had gathered.

I received a letter from the Iowa Department of Records in response to an enquiry I made several weeks ago concerning George's birth certificate. They needed more information to complete my request.

Wednesday August 21, 1996

After my morning nap, I finally called Noel Neil and discovered the phone number was incorrect. I felt I had wandered down a dead end street with three roadblocks: No address for Jack Larson, no birth certificate for George, and now the wrong number for Noel Neil. I have years of research background and have never had so many pathways blocked all at once. George said he could feel my intense frustration.

Tuesday August 27, 1996

Gary finally spoke to Matthew about my sexual relationship with George and indicated Matt did not appear to be upset. Gary informed me a topic as sensitive as having a sexual relationship with a spirit would take time to sink in.

Later, I contacted Los Angeles County to obtain a copy of George Reeves' autopsy report and found it would cost ninety-six dollars. The clerk indicated this fee was charged for all old reports. I felt the amount was excessive and decided to put the item on hold due to budget concerns.

Wednesday August 28, 1996

I phoned the Screen Actors Guild again and they gave me a newer phone number for Noel Neil. After speaking with the Guild, I called Noel and the number worked. I got her answering machine and the outgoing message went something like "she was off to the Daily Planet." I immediately hung up the phone because it made me laugh and George commented she still likes all the old memories. I then called back and left a message. I hoped she would return my call.

Following my brief message to Noel, George started talking about the good times they had together. George likes to keep positive feelings and memories flowing because Gary delves into the hard times of our past. Because we now share each other's emotions, George likes to balance it out with light-hearted banter. It then occurred to me, Noel would probably like to know George's spirit is here; that death is just a doorway and not a box in the ground.

Wednesday September 4, 1996

During today's session, Gary wanted more information regarding the first time George came to me in a dream when I was thirteen. He specifically wanted to know was there something else besides the dream that told me George Reeves was dead. The only other detail I recalled was just a strong inner knowing about his death.

Then the focus shifted to George's experience with the movie industry. As George talked about the Hollywood scene, I again realized the movie industry wasn't as glamorous from the inside as it looked from the outside. George indicated performers had to "prostitute" themselves both body and soul to get movie roles. You eventually ended up with parts of your personality dying.

Monday September 9, 1996

During session today, Gary focused on George's youth. At first, I felt George resisting Gary's questions because he didn't want to talk about that period of his life again. Finally, George opened up and spoke about his feelings concerning his mother's control over his life. The more George talked, the more my stomach hurt.

George said that the type of women he later became involved with were controlling like his mother. Eleanor, Toni, and Leonore all had George on their proverbial leash. I hoped I wasn't that type of woman. I know I'm a strong person and have always wanted a man who could be my equal, but at the same time I can take the lead when necessary.

George has told me I am nothing like the other women he's had in his life. We've had equal roles in all of our incarnations. In our past lives, I would often urge him toward the goals he needed to accomplish, but he said I was never controlling. We were partners in the truest sense. That disclosure came as a relief because I don't want to be anything like the controlling women he had during his life.

Gary then asked me how I was dealing with what was currently happening in my life. I told him at times I felt very lonely. I only have Matt to talk with and that's not as often as I would like. I can't talk to Duncan because he doesn't believe in the spirit world. Being unable to talk with someone about something so profound as what I am experiencing bothers me deeply.

Later, I ordered *Hollywood Kryptonite* from the publisher. They said it would be released September 16th, which was a date different from that which was reported in the newspaper. I found this interesting because the 16th has significance to George and me.

Tuesday September 9, 1996

During meditation, George wanted to show me a bit of his early life. I saw him riding on a train to Pasadena, California when he was about six years old. He was both excited and afraid by the adventure of moving to a new city.

In Pasadena, the neighborhood children made fun of George because Helen dressed him in short pants, which George referred to as his monkey suit.

George felt isolated because the neighborhood children didn't want anything to do with him. They called him "momma's boy." With the urging of his grandfather, George enrolled in a military academy to prove his manhood. Later, for the same reason, he took up boxing.

George said he always felt alone and isolated. As a celebrity he had to endure a lot of hard work and criticism. People always wanted to touch him. Sometimes they wanted to hit him. I felt his profound sadness.

I reflected on the similarity between Helen and Toni. Helen only gave conditional love, wanting everything done her way. Her control over George's life worked while he was young, but as he grew older, George had his own ideas about how he wanted to live.

Saturday September 14, 1996

A most unusual thing happened when Matt and I went to Gary's home to install the new modem in his computer. When we arrived, Gary's truck was in the driveway, a sign he was home. Matt knocked on the door but there was no answer. We waited awhile thinking he might be in the bathroom or somewhere else in the house, so we knocked again but still no answer.

We walked over to Gary's carpentry shop beside the house thinking he might be there but the door was locked. Matt and I then walked around the house, sat on the front steps for awhile and finally knocked again but still no answer. I thought Gary might have gone somewhere with Daryl. Perhaps he had forgotten we were coming over. We left a note in the door and went to lunch.

By the time we returned home, Gary had called and left a message. He had been at the house all along in the kitchen. He heard Pax the cat jump off the window perch signaling the cat heard something but didn't take notice and did not hear us knock.

The other odd thing that happened was we had two cellular phones in the car and did not think to call Gary. There must be a reason why we are having problems installing the modem. I again wondered whether something was trying to prevent the book from happening.

Monday September 16, 1996

George finally informed me there were dark forces interfering with the book project. He did not have to name names but I knew they had to be the infamous Toni and Eddie Mannix. George indicated Gary and I needed to protect ourselves from these negative forces by pooling our spiritual energy.

Later in the day, Matt called to set up another appointment to install the modem but the message did not record on Gary's answering machine and again he was home. This incident reinforced my feelings something unseen or malevolent was blocking the book project. It now appears more than ever we do need to connect psychically and pool our energies.

George indicated Gary should be aware of the negative forces and start protecting himself, especially when he and his team investigate hauntings. George feels Gary could be in a lot of danger. I should start using the banishing ritual Gary taught us in class to protect myself from these negative forces as well. George indicated that although I am being protected there are still forces being brought into my house by others, which could affect the book's progress. I felt if we are getting that much resistance then the book must really be important.

Thursday September 19, 1996

I'm finally beginning to remember my dreams again after a long lull. I dreamed about George, Gary, and myself sitting in a comfortable room talking and laughing about what we have been going through. We were all dressed in white and sitting in white wing backed chairs. There were only two of us because George and I had merged back into one soul.

Sunday September 22, 1996

I woke up with George talking to me about a major fight he and Toni had at the time of their break-up. Things between he and Toni were very strained because she was becoming more possessive. George hadn't seen Toni for some time because he had been out of town. After meeting Leonore Lemon in New York, George decided to end the relationship with Toni. He tried to be as kind to her as possible but she became upset and a yelling match ensued.

During the fight, Toni threw a few objects at George but he held his temper. Later, to reduce stress, he played The Game. He said he had a couple of drinks, went up to the bedroom and shot off the Lugar. He now knew because he ended the relationship with Toni there would be trouble with Eddie. Toni called a few times and tried to patch things up but George said the relationship was over.

A short time later, harassing calls began and I felt George's anger over the calls. George knew no matter what he did, there would be trouble because he had broken the pact with Eddie. Although Eddie had not come through with his part of the deal, he still did not like to be crossed.

Monday September 23, 1996

Duncan and I were getting ready to go back to St. Simon's Island, Georgia and I could hardly wait! With extra work all summer and my experiences with George, I knew I needed to rest and sort things out.

After getting a few things packed, I was off to see Gary for our last session before vacation. He regressed me again to the years between 1804 and 1869 and spent a lot of time delving into the relationship George and I had with him during that period. It became clear John was as possessive of me then as George is now. This did not prevent Robert, John, and Suzanne from having many good times together.

Although John drew the line with the ménage a trios, that did not prevent Robert and me from becoming lovers after John died. I could feel Suzanne loved Robert well enough to have shared a relationship with both him and John, but that arrangement would have been frowned upon in those days. I then wondered how a three-way relationship would have changed our later incarnations.

Revisiting The Truth And The Lies

We travel not for trafficking alone:
By hotter winds our fiery hearts are fanned:
For lust of knowing what should not be known,
We took the Golden Road to Samarkand.
—J. E. Flecker

TΣM

Thursday September 26, 1996

It felt so good to be back in St. Simon's. Once we had settled in and rested, we decided to drive to Savannah and do some sightseeing. After lunch and a leisurely stroll on the wharf, Duncan and I toured the Revolutionary War cemetery we'd visited last year, which was located in the center of the old city.

First, I went to William Stevens' gravesite and again had strong feelings of a presence. I then walked over to the MacIntosh graves and felt the same tingly sensations I'd felt the year before. Although, there were graves dated after the Revolutionary War, I could not find John or Suzanne Stevens' graves. I would probably need to contact the historical society in order to locate their gravesites.

Back in St. Simon's, I felt I needed to take the edge off my research endeavors so Duncan and I strolled on the catwalk outside our condominium and saw the most beautiful lunar eclipse. I could feel George's presence as I watched the orange glow of the eclipsing moon reflecting off the ocean's waters. After a long silence, George remarked that the eclipse was gorgeous. He said in time he would take me to other eclipses, which would be lovelier because we would finally be together.

Monday September 30, 1996

I was planning to go back to Savannah to do more research but because it was raining, and I'd had a dream the previous night about my being in an auto accident, I stayed on the island. There'd be plenty of vacation time remaining for research. So, if weather permits, I'll just relax and beach bum around on the island.

Tuesday October 1, 1996

It was cloudy again today but no rain in sight, so I took the chance and drove back to Savannah. This time I ended up at the central library, which had an extensive history section dating back centuries.

The library archivist steered me to a book on plantations where I found a plantation owned by a John Stevens. The book also contained 1850 census data, which listed all the names that had surfaced in our regressions. Although the names were the same, I still could not discern whether these were the actual people who appeared in my regression scenarios.

By the time I had completed my research for the day, it started to rain. As I was driving back to St. Simon's, a large truck passed me spraying gallons of water on the windshield. For a few seconds, I couldn't see where I was going and lost control of the car. After regaining control, I made it safely back to the condominium without any further problems, though my thoughts did flash back to the dream I'd had two nights before.

Thursday October 3, 1996

It was the last full day on the island and Duncan and I spent it at Fort Fredericka. The fort was used as a coastal lookout post during both the Revolutionary and Civil Wars. We had been there twice before, but because of time constraints, we could not see the Fort in detail. However, on this occasion we had plenty of time to look around.

Walking on one of the trails, an odd thing happened and I suddenly felt George staying very close to me. He said there were many spirits around and some were not happy. I then heard a voice coming from a spirit of an English soldier who had died there during the Revolutionary War. The spirit told me he was drunk and alone and had fallen into the Fredericka River and drowned.

I then heard two other spirits talking with George whose names were James and Thomas. They had been hiding on the island to escape the war when vigilantes found and murdered them. All the spirits wanted to know how George had attached himself to me. I found this experience very unusual and a bit unsettling because they wanted to attach themselves to someone like George had done. It appeared these spirits were stuck in time and I began to wonder if the way spirits are released from places is by attaching themselves to people.

It was apparent these spirits were attached to this place and could not accept they were dead. I became aware of several other spirits who had been murdered but none of them identified themselves. Although, I never felt I was in any serious danger because George was with me, I realized the need to call on my spirit guides for protection wherever I go.

As I was gearing up for the trip back to Cincinnati, I started wondering if the *Hollywood Kryptonite* book had arrived. George assured me it had. I was looking forward to reading it but at the same time, I felt a bit uneasy. I don't know if the uneasy feelings were George's or mine.

Friday October 4, 1996

After returning home, a letter had arrived from the researcher in Galesburg, Illinois but there was no book. I was surprised because George had assured me the book would be there and he's usually right.

The letter indicated there was no marriage listing for Helen in Galesburg, Illinois. Although, records from that period are sometimes sketchy and in an area where three states border, she could have been married in Iowa, Illinois, or Kentucky.

Saturday October 5, 1996

No sooner had I gotten back from St. Simon's I was in Gary's new course on Psychic Development. Matt came along because after class we were going to have lunch with Gary and a classmate, Gloria, to discuss the trip and then later Matt would try to install a new modem.

I felt rather uneasy in class because George remarked there were many spirits in the room and not all of them were good. We started class as usual with a short biography and then went into a meditation. In the meditation, I saw the three soldiers from Fort Fredericka again. They still appeared to be stuck and unhappy. They wanted to move on but didn't know how.

After the meditation, we separated into groups and performed a color transmitting telepathy exercise. Matt, Gloria, and I scored two out of three trials correctly.

After class, we had a lovely lunch and then went to Gary's home to hook up the modem. Again it didn't work! I feel there is something preventing us from connecting our modems and George insists its Eddie and Toni. The vibes inside Gary's house seemed very good, but there was something sinister outside because on the way in, George kept very close to me.

Sunday October 6, 1996

I could not believe it but *Hollywood Kryptonite* had been at the house all along. Duncan and I bought an exercise machine and had to bring it in through the front door. There between the storm and screen doors was the parcel containing the book! George had been right all along. George had told both Gary and I that Eddie Mannix looked like a bulldog. There on the book jacket was a picture of Eddie and sure enough, he did. In the first few chapters all the things George had told us, including Eddie's syndicate connection, were verified. Even though I'm seeing Gary tomorrow, I called and left a message about the book.

After opening the book to the center section containing pictures, George reacted immediately to a snapshot of his schnauzer, Sam. According to George, Toni had Sam kidnapped weeks before his murder. George loved that dog and the picture brought tears to our eyes.

As I read, I began feeling anxious. I didn't know if the feelings were George's or mine. I reassured George that no matter what the book revealed, I would always love him and nothing would change that fact. George kept saying he's sorry, but I didn't know what about. I told him he had witnessed all my mistakes and yet he is still with me. I guess we are somewhat alike in our insecurities.

Monday October 7, 1996

It was two o'clock in the morning and I was still reading. I could feel George's pain and embarrassment. I stopped reading and closed the book because George could no longer deal with those memories. It's like he's reliving the June 16th night all over again. I told him I loved him and none of the information makes any difference between us or ever will.

The book revealed more similarities between our lives. The first house my husband George Owens and I rented and the one George and Toni bought were both Cape Cod style houses. The backs of the two houses faced a hillside. And to top it off, George and I were both registered Republicans.

Later we had a two hour session with Gary. He spent most of the time talking with George about his relationships with Toni, Leonore, and Helen. The topic abruptly changed when George became upset over losing his dog, the lies about his father, and his birth name.

Wednesday October 9, 1996

I finally finished *Hollywood Kryptonite*. The book's version of George's death was somewhat different from what he had revealed to us. George stands by his version of what happened that June night and indicated there were many untruths in the book.

The acknowledgment section of the book revealed there was a Super Museum in Metropolis, Illinois. George wants me to go to the museum, talk to Jim Hambrick the curator, and find out what he knows about George's life. If I go, I hope Gary can come along.

Thursday October 10, 1996

I discovered this morning that Duncan had been in my computer files and printed one of my business letters. I don't know how he reacted to the letter because we haven't talked at all about what is happening with me. He knows I'm writing a book but he doesn't know what it's about. He would not respond well if he found out.

The fundamentalist church Duncan attends would think I'm possessed by the devil or something silly like that. I know my current situation with George would lead to problems in my marriage, but I have to follow my soul's journey and my love. With all I have experienced throughout my life, I know I'm on the right road and cannot turn back.

Tuesday October 15, 1996

George spent most of the session today discussing the inaccuracies and contradictions in *Hollywood Kryptonite*. He indicated the authors did not present an accurate portrayal of who he was and George stressed he had never lied to us about his life. I feel the inaccuracies and contradictions will be cleared up when I go to the Super Museum and interview Jim Hambrick. I also feel Jim's input could be critical to our book.

Wednesday October 16, 1996

I finally called Jim Hambrick at the Super Museum and it appeared he might be a good connection. He agreed that there were many inaccuracies in *Hollywood Kryptonite*. After putting out a few subtle suggestions, I discovered Jim might be open to the idea that George and I have a psychic connection. Jim remarked that over the years he too has had unusual things happen in his life.

What topped off the conversation was Jim knew both Jack Larson and Noel Neil quite well. I felt that through him I might be able to get Jack's address and phone number. I was so excited after talking with Jim. I hoped Gary could make the trip with me!

Thursday October 17, 1996

Gary appeared very excited about taking a trip to the Super Museum. He thinks interviewing Jim could help validate the information George had disclosed to us. If everything goes as planned, we will be taking a trip to Metropolis, Illinois in two weeks. It seems like a long way off.

George and I have some apprehension about interviewing Jim. This will be the first time we'll have to produce information for someone other than Gary.

Tuesday October 22, 1996

Gary informed George that their Tuesday night telepathic experiment was successful; he felt George's presence. George said the experiment revealed Toni's spirit was very active, especially at the Benedict Canyon house. The reason she was so active was because George and I are together and the book project is underway.

I could tell after George's disclosure that Gary seemed somewhat skeptical. Gary explained that, although he had felt George's image in their experiments, he was still not sure it was really George Reeves. He said the images could be coming from my own psychic projections and if it's really George's spirit why couldn't George make himself known outside of the experiments?

George prompted me to relax so he could separate from me. I became aware of an energy outline around my head and shoulders. The outline then separated from my body, emerged outwards toward Gary, and then moved back into my body. When I opened my eyes, Gary looked stunned. He said he felt a strong energy emanating from me. He saw a physical manifestation around my head but didn't understand what was happening. He abruptly ended the session and said he wanted me fully grounded before I left his office.

After leaving Gary's office, I went home and fell fast asleep. The experience had totally exhausted me.

Saturday October 26, 1996

As I sat in class, I felt the other students brought many spirits into the room, but I could not tell whether they were good or bad. The spirit energies interfered with my telepathic exercises.

After leaving class, I had an afterthought and went back to ask Gary a question. On the way home, there were two auto accidents right in front of me. If I had not gone back to ask Gary a question, I felt I would have been involved in one of these accidents. I felt George had been looking out for me.

Monday October 28, 1996

We had another book meeting on the heels of Gary reading a few chapters of *Hollywood Kryptonite*. Gary had a few pointed questions for George regarding his drinking. Gary also asked why George's friends did not help him get good parts in the movies after the war. George said flatly, "It's a cutthroat industry."

Experiencing Subtle Truths

Tis strange—But true; for truth is always strange, stranger than fiction.
—Lord Byron

TΣM

Gary

After four months of working with Jean, I felt I was beginning to understand the psychological dynamics in her personality structure. I was positive Jean unconsciously created the George Reeves alter personality and it functioned as a coping mechanism. Although Jean believed the alter personality was the spirit of George Reeves, I perceived this belief to be a delusion.

Jean, however, was convinced the past-life regressions proved she and the late actor had lived many previous lifetimes together. This assumption, coupled with her belief that she and George were twin souls, propelled her to search for similarities between their lives.

Jean felt that, because she and George were twin souls, they had many life parallels. I felt that she projected onto the alter personality the similarities she wanted. Once these similarities were incorporated into the alter personality they were communicated back to Jean as if they were coming from the spirit of George Reeves.

Jean had projected numerous parallels onto the alter personality (see Appendix B). It was my opinion, however, that what Jean considered as parallels, were, at best, very loose fitting similarities, which she had confabulated and projected into her George Reeves delusion.

Jean explained she and the spirit George Reeves spent weeks compiling the list of parallels. This was evidence she and the alter personality had colluded in creating these fabricated similarities, lending more support to her delusional beliefs. In my opinion, Jean probably obtained these parallels from pictures and biographies of the late actor.

To test the hypothesis that Jean had read biographies of George Reeves, I requested she loan me one so I could authenticate the list of parallels. She immediately informed me there were no biographies written on George Reeves. Although a man named Jim Beaver was in the process of writing one, it had not yet been published.

She further explained it was difficult finding information on George Reeves because he was very private about his personal life. The only materials she was able to locate concerned his acting career and his role as Superman. I was suddenly faced with an informational void. Normally in these cases, people collect vast amounts of material in order to support their delusions. If I was going to chisel away at her delusional system, I needed to find relevant information on the late actor. However, before I could begin my investigation, Jean informed me another voice came to her while meditating in a local park. She referred to the voice as the Old One and said it was softer than George's voice. The voice informed her we were on the right spiritual path and to continue our journey.

Had Jean's personality split yet again? Just as that thought crossed my mind, George emerged and informed me the Old One was a transcendent master whose name was Miracle. Miracle was a member of George's spiritual counsel, which he referred to as the Old Ones. According to George, the Old Ones were spirit guides existing in higher spiritual dimensions and were positive forces that would be assisting us with the book project.

After George's disclosure, I concluded the Old One was probably a split-off fragment of Jean's personality. Even though Miracle was part of Jean's personality, it appeared on the surface this new personality was different from George in that Miracle did not appear to have a coherent life history. Although different from George, I found it interesting that Miracle was also a male, indicating another part of Jean's personality was also gender specific.

Based on what George had explained about the Old Ones, it was now clear Jean and George had colluded in creating Miracle. Unlike George, Miracle did not verbally communicate to me through Jean. Although they said Miracle existed, I had no verbal evidence to the fact.

I began feeling that Jean was using George and this new

transcendent master to incorporate me into her delusional system by continuing to insist we write a book together. Jean's book-writing obsession began shortly before the June 16th meeting in my office and was now becoming more intense. She kept stressing George wanted us to write a book about their twin soul relationship, the love they have toward each other, and the many lifetimes they had lived.

Though I was very resistant to the book idea, it intrigued me that Jean had projected it onto the personality she had created. It appeared once Jean had projected the thought of writing a book onto George Reeves, he began owning the thought and eventually the idea became part of his overall personality structure.

I considered that if Jean could project information onto the personality then maybe I could too. If I could facilitate information transfer onto this personality, it would give me an understanding of how diffused their ego boundaries were. It would also indicate how susceptible Jean was to external influences. If I was able to penetrate her ego boundaries, then probably so could others.

The telepathic experiment I eventually constructed tested whether I could transmit information to Jean through George. If I telepathically transmitted thoughts to George, could Jean pick up those thoughts as well? In addition, I wanted to learn whether I could telepathically connect with George at a particular time and whether he could come into my awareness at will.

As it happened, aspects of the first question were answered before I had the chance to test it. George or Jean had already picked up my thoughts concerning the experiment and through Jean, George informed me he would be interested in trying the experiment.

At first, I was stunned and wondered if I had unconsciously given some clues about the experiment. I reasoned that because of Jean's diffused ego boundaries she must have noticed some subtleties I was giving off. Another possibility was my psychic defenses could have been relaxed and with her diffused ego boundaries, she was able to mesh with me telepathically and pick up my thoughts. In any case, I felt the first experiment was already underway. Jean or George was beginning to connect with me on a psychic level.

I decided to perform the second experiment and have George come to me clairvoyantly while I was in a meditative state enabling me to see him clearly. Jean and I decided on a date and time when we were free from external constraints so we could go into a meditative state without interruption. The meditative state would allow George to leave Jean and come to me clairvoyantly.

At the assigned date and time, I placed a picture of the actor George Reeves on a table and focused on the picture for about thirty minutes. I closed my eyes and began to meditate, which cleared my mind of thoughts and allowed my psychic defenses to relax. I was then in a receptive state to allow George to come into my inner awareness.

For several weeks, Jean, George and I attempted to connect clairvoyantly but all the experiments ended in failure. Finally, one night several weeks later, I easily moved into a deeper meditative state. I felt entranced and my mind was totally blank.

On the horizon, I saw a green field surrounded by lush green trees. The sky was sunny and a few translucent clouds drifted through the bright blue background. I saw a man in period clothes. He wore a blue-tailed coat with a white top hat. I was engaged in a conversation with him but was not conscious of what was being said. The scene lasted for only a short period when I realized I was trying to come out of the meditation but couldn't. I continued struggling and finally managed to get back to ordinary consciousness. I felt very groggy.

I later discovered the experiment was a success because George explained he left Jean while she was sleeping. If he tried to leave her while awake or even in a meditative state, their spiritual bond was so strong that it was hard for him to separate. The amount of energy George used to separate from Jean depleted his energy supply, which prevented him from attaining a good psychic connection with me.

George said he appeared to me in period clothes to show me how Jean saw him as John Stevens. He also said that when he came into my awareness I began resisting his contact, which shortened the length of the experience. I found this detail interesting because when George first came into my awareness I was calm. Then I realized what was happening and resisted, concerned about possession. Jean and George assured me possession was not possible because they were twin souls and spiritually connected only with each other.

TΣM

I wondered if I had imagined the scene in which George was dressed in period clothes. I reasoned I could have created the scene out of the accumulated details from Jean's past-life regressions. On the other hand, I wondered if George had literally transferred his image into my awareness. In any case, something profound was happening and I was at a loss to explain it.

Before I had the chance to fit together the puzzle pieces, Jean and George began stressing we needed to get started writing the book because the Old Ones were waiting to assist us. Jean indicated writing her part of the book would be easy because she had been keeping a diary of her experiences with George Reeves. Therefore, to appease Jean, I wrote a few paragraphs, showed them to her and she appeared satisfied.

My intention was to placate Jean long enough to figure out a strategy to move her away from her book writing obsession. Before I could come up with a suitable intervention, however, Jean called and informed me someone had recently written a book on George's life. I was relieved to hear the news and hoped this biography would quell Jean's interest in co-authoring a book with me.

Jean had read a newspaper release that a biography on George Reeves, entitled *Hollywood Kryptonite,* was slated to be published in November, about three months away. George told Jean we had been sucker-punched and she asked me what that meant. I explained in boxing and street fighting a sucker punch is when your opponent hits you without fair warning.

What was astonishing, Jean didn't know what sucker-punched meant, but the alter personality did. This was a surprise because sucker-punched is a term boxers would know and George had informed me earlier he took up boxing to prove his manhood. I assumed Jean must have read the term in one of the articles she had on the late actor, repressed it, and later projected it into the alter personality where it now surfaced as his original knowledge.

This repression process is called cryptomnesia and is an experience many of us have had throughout our lives. Cryptomnesia often occurs when we have forgotten information we have read or heard and the information surfaces as our own novel idea or ideas. I was sure this was what was occurring with Jean in reference to the sucker-punched comment.

I was elated by the forthcoming George Reeves biography because it would help validate the information Jean had disclosed about the late actor. I could use this information with the aid of therapeutic maneuvers to challenge Jean's delusional system and help her reclaim fragments of her personality.

Jean wasted no time contacting the publisher and ordering the biography. The publisher indicated *Hollywood Kryptonite* would be on the market in October rather than November, and Jean should have her copy sometime during that month.

The forthcoming book, however, dissuaded neither Jean nor George from their own book idea. In fact, George said our book would be different in that it would focus on the spiritual relationship between him and Jean.

I suddenly realized writing a book with Jean would give me access to her diary, which would in turn yield insight into how she had constructed the George Reeves personality. I was ready to scrap the few paragraphs I had written and start work on a short introduction. This would demonstrate to Jean I was serious about the book, and put me on the fast track to her diary.

Jean's son Matthew had been scavenging modems from old computers trying to find a model that would work in mine. After several months of frustration, Matt found a new modem he thought would work and scheduled a Saturday morning in mid-September to install it.

That Saturday morning I waited for Jean and Matthew's arrival while working in the kitchen. I patiently waited for several hours and they neither showed up nor called, which was very uncharacteristic for Jean. About one o'clock in the afternoon, I decided to work on an unfinished project in my carpentry shop. When I opened the front door, a piece of paper fell out. I unfolded the paper and to my surprise, it was a note from Jean and Matthew. The note indicated they had been to the house and had knocked several times but no one answered.

I found the note quite puzzling because I had been home all morning and had not heard them knock. The only noise I heard was Pax the cat jumping off his perch. I called and left a message on Jean's answering machine indicating I had been home all along and had not heard their knock.

Later that day Jean and I talked by phone. She indicated they had knocked several times on the front door, walked around the house and then knocked again. She informed me George kept telling her the spirits of Toni and Eddie Mannix were interfering with our book project and that's why I didn't hear them knock.

I felt I was probably preoccupied at the time and unconsciously tuned out extraneous sounds. Furthermore, our computer problems had nothing to do with the sinister forces, but rather old machinery.

TΣM

I realized that because Jean's chapters would come directly from her diary, creating a readable narrative would be a daunting task. To sort through the incoherent ramblings, out of sequence afterthoughts, and sporadic thought fragments from the dairy, it was evident we needed editorial help.

Jean and I discussed our financial options and finding an editor we had to pay was out of the question. We also needed someone we knew and trusted because of the sensitive nature of the subject matter. With that in mind I suggested we consider my life-partner Daryl, whom had impeccable editing skills. Jean and George were delighted with the suggestion. They had met Daryl on several occasions in his vitamin shop and liked him very much.

After earning a degree in Psychology, Daryl had pursued graduate work in Health Management and eventually opened a vitamin and supplement business next to my office. Shortly thereafter, he and I formed a consulting group, assisting people in the development of healthy lifestyle management.

Daryl and I also started a psychic research team, investigating paranormal occurrences in the Cincinnati area. With his varied background and editorial skills, both Jean and I thought Daryl would be the perfect editor for the book project.

Once I had Jean's okay to bring Daryl aboard, I approached him with our proposal. Daryl recalled that a psychic he'd visited two years earlier had predicted he would be involved in a project with a woman from the medical field with issues around death and dying. This prompted him to agree to our proposal without too much deliberation. I brought him up to date on the case and he was amazed with the accuracy of the psychic's predictions as well as the physical similarities between Jean and the late actor, George Reeves. Daryl said he had been a Superman fan growing up.

Now that we had an editor, I began outlining the introduction but soon found myself having great difficulty explaining the twin soul concept. I knew very little about the topic and didn't even believe the phenomenon existed. I decided to give Jean the benefit of the doubt and Daryl and I began researching the topic.

To adequately research the twin soul topic, I felt I needed a respite away from the influences of Jean and the alter personality George Reeves. As it turned out, I got the time I needed because Jean and her husband Duncan took a vacation to St. Simon's Island, Georgia. I would have over a week to investigate the topic of twin souls and to review Jean's case history.

Daryl informed me he had come up with something in his twin soul research. He'd found a web site in which a husband and wife claimed they were twin souls. I, too, had some progress. It occurred to me that if anyone should know about the twin soul phenomenon it would be my good friend Bunny Hall. She's a voracious reader of the spiritual and paranormal.

I set up a luncheon date with Bunny and met her at the University Hospital where she worked. Over lunch, I discussed Jean's case as much as my professional ethics would allow. I explained how I thought Jean had constructed George out of a need to cope with the many losses in her life.

Bunny quickly noted that Jean's experience was not necessarily a delusion. She explained that many people have experiences with spirits, and in Jean's case it happened to be George Reeves. In fact, Bunny had recently read a book on twin souls and, after weighing all the facts, felt that Jean's twin soul experience with George Reeves was probably true.

By week's end, Bunny had loaned me the book entitled *Twin Souls: Finding Your True Spiritual Partner,* by Patricia Joudry and Maurie D. Pressman. As I read the book I was very skeptical of Joudry's explanation of the twin soul phenomenon and the cases she presented to support her argument. Nevertheless, the book did provide a novel discussion on two other topics: soul mates and group souls.

In references to the twin soul phenomenon, the book went into a lengthy metaphysical discourse on how twin souls emerge from divine energy. From this energy, the soul divides into separate parts and these parts continue to divide throughout eons until the soul separates into two final segments of masculine and feminine. This final division of masculine and feminine occurs just before the two halves of the soul merge back together again, in a state of perfect unity. What was surprising about Joudry's explanation was how similar it was to what the alter personality George Reeves had said. I wondered if Jean had read this book.

TΣM

Jean's vacation went fast and before I knew it, she was back in Cincinnati. *Hollywood Kryptonite* had arrived and Jean immediately delved into it. Within days, she was sitting in my office discussing it. She said that according to George much of the book's information was inaccurate.

I mentioned I had recently read a book by Patricia Joudry and Maurie Pressman entitled *Twin Souls* and asked if she had heard of it. Jean said she had not. I commented on how Joudry's explanation of twin souls was very similar to what George had revealed, which prompted Jean to remark that this should confirm her twin soul relationship with George. I then asked if she was interested in reading it and she emphatically declined stating her interest was *Hollywood Kryptonite*.

I interjected Daryl had found one case on the Internet of a husband and wife who claimed they were twin souls but he was continuing to search for other cases. Jean suddenly reacted very negatively saying her relationship with George was not like any other relationship; theirs was unique and different. She quickly shifted back to *Hollywood Kryptonite*.

After discussing several more inaccuracies, Jean handed me the book. *Hollywood Kryptonite* was a blue book with a multi-colored dust jacket displaying three pictures. There was a large picture I recognized immediately as George Reeves in his Superman costume and two smaller pictures of a man and a woman, which turned out to be Eddie and Toni Mannix.

I could not take my eyes off the picture of Eddie Mannix because there was something familiar about it and then realized what it was. George had mentioned earlier that Eddie looked like a bulldog and the picture on the dust cover did resemble a bulldog. I wondered if Jean had seen a picture of Eddie in one of her movie books and projected that detail onto the alter personality George Reeves. However, recently she had loaned me all the books she had collected on George Reeves and I did not remember seeing any pictures of Eddie Mannix. I felt Jean must have seen a picture of him somewhere and had forgotten it, another example of cryptomnesia.

Jean mentioned that in the acknowledgment section of Hollywood Kryptonite the authors had interviewed a man named Jim Hambrick who was an authority on George Reeves and Superman. She also pointed out, Jim was the curator of the Super Museum in a town called Metropolis, Illinois and chuckled at the name of the town. She said she was going to contact Jim soon.

Within the week, Jean had contacted Jim Hambrick by phone and according to her, they hit it off, talking at length about their interest in the late actor and the inaccuracies in

Hollywood Kryptonite.

Jean informed Jim we were also writing a book about George Reeves but it was spiritual in nature and very different from *Hollywood Kryptonite.*

She indicated we needed specific information regarding George Reeves' life and felt his in-depth knowledge would be a great value to our book project. She asked if he was open to being interviewed and he said he was. She closed the conversation by telling Jim she would get back in touch with him to schedule a date and time to meet.

Jean later asked if I could free up my schedule to accompany her to Metropolis, Illinois and interview Jim Hambrick. She stressed that both she and George thought Jim would probably have information and pictures we could use in our book. I checked my schedule and the weekend of November first and second was open.

I felt meeting Jim Hambrick would afford me the opportunity to ask specific questions regarding George Reeves in the hope of putting some cracks into Jean's delusional system. Jean had given many specific details regarding the late actor and now I would have the chance to challenge the information. By subtly challenging her delusional belief the spirit of George Reeves was with her, I could conceivably move her away from that delusion and toward personality integration.

TΣM

I decided before taking the trip to Metropolis, Illinois I would reevaluate Jean's psychological status. I needed to have a clear picture of her personality structure so I could ask Jim Hambrick the right questions.

I reevaluated Jean's personality in reference to psychotic disorders and again found no evidence. Although she hears the voice of the personality George Reeves it appears he communicates with her in normal conversational patterns. She also hears the voice of the transcendent master, Miracle. As with George it appears Miracle communicates with her in a similar manner and not with stereophonic, disorganized, incoherent, or otherwise schizophrenic speech patterns. There was no flattened affect to her voice, which would have indicated severe depressive reactions. Although there was a lack of psychotic features clustering around a specific syndrome, Jean did seem to manifest delusional thinking in reference to the actor George Reeves.

Jean's case also had marked features of Dissociative Identity Disorder. This disorder usually causes severe psychological, occupational, and social impairment, but Jean was unaffected in these domains. In Jean's case, dissociation emerges as a coping strategy to deal with stress and to escape psychological, emotional, and physical pain.

In non-pathological situations, dissociation is a primary feature of drug-induced states, mystical states, and religious trance states. Because Jean is psychologically, occupationally, and socially functional, there does appear to be a mystical quality to her dissociative experience. There is also a pathological quality; hence this case is very perplexing.

In an attempt to get beyond this perplexity, I constructed an experiment. If George Reeves could come into my awareness in a meditative state then shouldn't Jean be able to manifest him physically outside of a meditative state? If Jean could not manifest George, then this would prove he was a delusion.

In session, I asked George that since he was able to transfer his image into my awareness in a meditative state, then why couldn't he appear to me physically. I was utterly unprepared for what happened next.

Jean smiled and fell into a long silence. Next, Jean swallowed hard and looked straight into my eyes. I felt chills surge through my body. I was transfixed by her stare, could not look away, and felt paralyzed.

She then closed her eyes and a grayish-white shadow radiated around her. This shadowy radiation slowly began to take form and move out from Jean's body a few inches. The radiation continued to emerge a few more inches and ultimately took on the form of a hazy George Reeves. Jean appeared to be in a trance, with eyes closed and her face expressionless. It was apparent the personality had taken over Jean's body to show me what I had asked.

Abruptly, without a noticeable personality switch, the manifestation was gone and Jean was back to her normal self. I tried to keep my professional composure as I was seriously unnerved by what I had witnessed. I had expected nothing to happen, and now I had to consider the possibility of spirit possession.

George continued, calmly disclosing how spiritual energy could be molded into any form one imagines. He explained by using imagination and willpower, spiritual energy could be influenced in a variety of ways, or could create anything the soul desires. It was apparent in some way Jean had molded her spiritual energy to create the appearance of George Reeves in the shadowy energetic manifestation. Although, the manifestation was not as detailed or in the vivid colors I had experienced in the clairvoyant experiments, something profoundly physical had happened.

I later wondered whether Jean had used what psychics call ectoplasm to manifest George Reeves. Although still not certain what had transpired, I had trouble believing in Jean's construct of twin souls. I was ready to set the experience aside for the time and focus on the trip to Metropolis, Illinois and the interview with Jim Hambrick. I had accumulated a loose list of open-ended questions that I would ask Jim, hoping to elicit the information needed to challenge Jean's delusion that she was the twin soul of the late actor George Reeves.

The Awakening

The real voyage of discovery consists not in seeking new landscapes but in having new eyes . . .
—Marcel Proust

TΣM

Gary

It was a chilly Friday morning on November 1st, when Jean and I left for Metropolis, Illinois. I was excited to meet and interview Jim Hambrick. He was the person who had the information I needed to dismantle Jean's delusional system. The six-hour drive also gave me the opportunity to observe Jean in a non-clinical setting. As it turned out, she got the chance to relate to me in a different context as well. She was curious where I grew up and why I became a psychotherapist. I answered her many questions as best as I could while also keeping a professional distance.

We finally crossed the Ohio River from Paducah, Kentucky into Illinois. The land was flat on both sides of the river revealing the water worn terrain of centuries of erosion along the riverbanks. We turned onto an exit ramp leading down a sparsely tree-covered highway with autumn colors creating a warm comfortable atmosphere.

Jean and I registered at the motel, went to our rooms, and got ready to meet Jim Hambrick for our five o'clock interview. We drove down the tree lined main highway to Metropolis, a small Ohio River town with its first casino gambling boat.

There were signs of construction throughout the town indicating the casino's revenues were upgrading the town's financial coffers. The Super Museum was located on a corner across from a large Superman statue, standing watchfully over a small common in front of the courthouse and city hall. The Super Museum was housed on the first floor of an old two-story redbrick building. We entered and found it partitioned into two sections. The outer section was a small cluttered gift shop and the back section was the museum area.

Sitting on a stool behind the gift shop counter next to a turnstile signifying the museum's entrance was Jim Hambrick. Jim was rather tall, with long brown hair, probably in his late thirties or early forties with a pleasant smile. We chatted for several minutes in brief introduction and Jim invited us to go through the museum.

Jean went into the museum first. I waited for a few minutes chatting with Jim about our book project, setting up the tape recorder, and taking out a yellow pad preparing for the interview. I noticed the gift shop was well lit, but chilly, so I kept my jacket on. After concluding the conversation, I entered the museum, which was also cool, but unlike the gift shop, it was poorly lit.

Jim had collected a variety of relics and memorabilia from Superman as well as other Superheroes. I noticed a Superman costume in a glass case with an appraisal value of sixty-five thousand dollars. I was shocked at first, but then realized collectors would pay any price for a part of a collection they did not have. As I meandered through the museum I noticed a life mask of George Reeves. I became fascinated with how the eyes appeared to follow me.

The museum was a collection of anything and everything that pertained to Superman and Superhero characters, ranging from materials used on movie sets to matchboxes and plastic toy guns. I was amazed with all the items Jim had collected over the years pertaining to these Superheroes. After viewing all the exhibits, I returned to the gift shop, continued the conversation with Jim, and waited for Jean's return.

Jean

After entering the museum area, I was met with a full range of memories and memorabilia. There was a collection of items from the Superman productions, which included the early serials with Kirk Alyn, to Super Boy and Super Girl. I browsed through several displays and happened upon some interesting memorabilia.

Emotions began rising as George and I took it all in. I began to know things I hadn't known before and I kept returning to a costume on a mannequin display, which purported to have been worn by George. George kept saying there was something wrong with it.

Gary

I waited patiently talking with Jim, but after Jean's long absence, I became concerned and searched for her. I found her gazing at a mounted costume looking puzzled. When I inquired what was wrong, George came out and said he had not worn the costume.

Intrigued, I pointed out another nearby display and asked George whether he had worn that costume. He said he wore that one in the early years of the Superman series. I asked why it was gray, and he explained that those episodes were shot in black and white. Later on, the studio changed to color costumes for color shooting.

I pointed out yet another costume in a glass case, appraised at sixty-five thousand dollars, and asked George if he had worn that one. He studied the costume for several minutes and then said he had worn it but it had been re-stitched.

After looking around a bit more, we went back to the gift counter where Jim was waiting. I turned on the tape recorder and began the interview.

I gave Jim a brief history of the events leading up to our decision to make the trip to interview him. I explained how a month before working with Jean I suddenly had an urge to read a James Dean biography, which was unusual because I had no interest in actors. I felt Dean's biography had prepared me to work with a case involving the actor George Reeves.

Jim sat with a smirk that indicated there was more to the Dean story than I realized. He explained there was a connection between George Reeves and James Dean. James Dean was a friend of Jack Larson, who played the young reporter Jimmy Olsen in the Superman series. I struggled to remember Jimmy Olsen from the TV series because as a child I neither liked nor watched Superman. I felt the connection between reading James Dean's biography and Dean being a friend of Jack Larson was synchronistic and wondered what it meant metaphorically.

Jim shared with us how George's death was devastating to him as well as many other boys in the 1950's. Out of his feelings of devastation and loss, Jim began collecting memorabilia on George Reeves, Superman, and other Superheroes.

At this point, I felt I needed to disclose Jean's connection with George Reeves, but did not know how Jim would react. I explained

Jean believes George Reeves is her twin soul and clarified what twin souls were. I then pointed out that, according to Jean, George's spirit came to her shortly after he died when she was thirteen, and has been with her ever since. I told Jim that the book we were writing is about their twin soul relationship and their many shared lifetimes. I said how I'd been able to talk with George through Jean, and how George has disclosed many details about his life. I then suggested if Jim wanted to talk to George, he could do so through Jean.

Jim's eyebrows furrowed and his face became flush. He turned toward Jean and confronted her. I stepped back to observe the interaction. I was especially interested in how Jean would react. Jim told her flatly he had dealt with charlatans before and if she were a fraud, George Reeves fans all over the world would destroy her.

I felt Jean's delusions around George Reeves would begin to crumble under the pressure and condemnation Jim Hambrick was leveling at her. However, after several minutes of Jim's constant berating and angry rebuke of Jean's spiritual connection with George, Jean appeared unfazed. She stood her ground and he rolled back his condescending rhetoric.

I was surprised Jean did not buckle under Jim. I could not understand how she kept her delusions intact after such an attack on her integrity. To diffuse the emotionally charged atmosphere, I calmly interjected that, regardless of what Superman fans thought, Jean believes her experience is real.

Jim began to cool down.

Superman outfit worn by George Reeves, valued at $65,000. Jean amazed the museum's curator by telling him that George told her the costume had been re-stitched.

Jim opened several George Reeves picture albums and Jean browsed the photos. She was able to identify people in the photos as well as the context in which the photographs had been taken. She whispered to me she was feeling a variety of George's emotions.

After reviewing the albums and sundry memorabilia, we began wrapping up the interview. Jim said if we returned the next day, he would show us more photo albums, and additional information including George's autopsy report.

With the tape recorder still running, I informed Jim I needed clarification on something George had told me through Jean. I explained that George had indicated the Superman costume on the mannequin next to the gray costume was one he had not worn. George also pointed out the costume in the display case appraised at sixty-five thousand dollars had been re-stitched.

The blood drained from Jim's face. "You're right," he said. "Only two people in the world know that—me and my insurance agent." He got off the stool and told us to wait a minute.

Jim returned with two Superman costumes in plastic bags and hung them on a revolving sweatshirt rack. Jean inspected the costumes closely and then George came out. George told us he had worn the two costumes in the last years they shot the Superman series.

Again, Jim was impressed and said, "That's right." Jim then brought out another item, a certificate from Pope Pius XII.

Baffled by what had just taken place, I asked George when did he have an audience with Pope Pius? George explained how one year he and Toni went to Rome and met the Pope. At the conclusion of that meeting, Pope Pius gave him the certificate.

I inspected the certificate closely and could tell by the brownish discoloration along the edges it had been framed. I asked George where he had hung the certificate. He said it was not hung at all; that he'd kept it atop the dresser in his bedroom. I turned to Jim for confirmation. He said this was correct.

George asked where the cross was. Startled, Jim said he knew nothing about a cross. George explained how some boys he had helped gave him the cross in appreciation, and that he always kept it with the certificate. Jim indicated he would inquire if anyone knew anything about the cross.

I was blown away. I wondered how Jean could've known all these intricate details, even some of which Jim was admittedly unaware.

Trying to put a rational spin on what I had just witnessed, I packed up my attaché case and started walking toward the gift shop's front entrance, when Jim asked Jean what about "the game."

Jean had no idea what Jim meant by "the game." The only game we knew anything about was the game George Reeves played with the Lugar, which we'd already discussed with Jim. Jean and I knew Jim must have been referring to a different game.

Jean

We left the Super Museum for the day and went to a locally approved restaurant for dinner. I felt George more than I ever had before. He was very pleased and kept telling me to relax, that he would take care of things.

Gary asked if George had told me about the game Jim had mentioned. I told him I still had no idea what the game was. We knew the game wasn't the one George played with the Lugar because Jim and I had already discussed that.

We ate dinner and chatted about the day and before parting ways, we agreed to meet for breakfast.

Later, I called Duncan and told him what I could about the trip. I left out many details because he would have gotten his minister to exorcise the demons from me. It was becoming clear that our paths were moving in very different directions.

When I finally had time to relax on the bed, I realized it was the first time I had talked to George alone all day. I beseeched him to tell me about the game. He told me to sleep and he would let me know later. George said I had his undying love and that I knew he wouldn't let me down. With that reassurance, I turned off the light and fell immediately to sleep.

Gary

After our meal, I laid in bed, my mind racing. I got up, walked around the room feeling confused, unsettled, antsy. I was baffled over what I had just witnessed and felt my assumptions, hypotheses, and theories were crumbling before my eyes. I knew if I didn't talk to someone I was going to explode. I called Daryl.

Daryl and I discussed many possibilities about what could be happening with Jean. One possibility I did not want to entertain was that George Reeves was not a delusion of Jean's, but a real spirit just as my friend Bunny had said. This concept did not fit into my current paradigm, but somehow I knew I had to change my thinking.

Jean

George woke me at 2 a.m. and while snuggling in his arms he told me what the game was. It was a hide-and-seek game, whoever found the item was "it" and I knew that had to be right. I returned peacefully to sleep with the happiest of dreams.

Gary

I awoke early the next morning anticipating the day and called Jean. She informed me during the night George had revealed what "the game" was and she would tell me over breakfast.

Later at breakfast Jean disclosed that, in the early years of filming the Superman series, George and another actor played a hide-and-seek game on the set with a particular sex toy, a dildo. That was the game Jim had referred to the previous night.

I listened to Jean with skepticism. I knew she somehow had information on the Superman costumes, but this "dildo" game sounded farfetched. I assumed I had finally cornered her and believed Jim would validate that assumption.

When we arrived at the museum, Jim was waiting for us. He had two stools pulled close to the gift shop counter and several more photo albums for us to review. Jean browsed the albums and stopped at a picture of George Reeves' Benedict Canyon house. I inspected the photo and noticed the Cape Cod house was almost identical to what George had described, but I also noticed some slight differences. When I inquired about the differences, Jim explained the house had gone through several renovations over the years.

Jean

Jim brought up the inaccuracies in *Hollywood Kryptonite*. We discussed how the authors portrayed George in a very negative light. Jim said that most people who knew George personally did not like the book's negative portrayal.

Later, Jim brought out the autopsy report. I felt apprehensive about looking at it. When I started to read the report, I immediately felt George tighten his grip as a deep sadness came over me. Up to this point, George had stayed in the background. I found an interesting item in the report and pointed it out to Gary. If George had been the drinker many said he was, then his liver would have begun to show some signs of damage. The autopsy report indicated there was no liver damage at all.

Jim then showed us the autopsy photos. As he handed them to me, Gary asked if I was okay. Nodding "yes," I accepted the plastic sheets containing the photographs. Then a tidal wave of grief washed over me. George gripped my body like a vise and tears started to flow—I could not tell whether they were his or mine. I had to move away from the pictures and collect my thoughts.

As a nurse, I had seen many autopsy reports and photos. I have cared for patients with terrible wounds—grotesque, real-life, full-color, putrid wounds much worse than those depicted in George's autopsy photos, but never have I been so struck as this. It was at that moment I knew George and I were merging into one.

There was no revulsion upon seeing the photos—my training had taken care of that—just soul-wrenching grief. It took me quite some time to compose myself. When I returned to the counter I could no longer bring myself to look at the photos.

Gary

After Jean regained her composure, it was time for us to leave. I thanked Jim for his time and help. I stepped away from the counter allowing Jean and Jim to talk alone. Browsing at some souvenirs, I kept close enough to hear what they were discussing.

Jean told Jim what George had revealed to her about the game he'd mentioned the previous night. Jim's head jerked back in surprise and he told Jean she was absolutely correct. I couldn't figure out how Jean knew such detailed information about the late actor, but I refused to believe it came from a spirit. There had to be some other explanation.

We asked Jim if we could return in the spring for a second interview and he said that would be fine. Then we left the museum and headed back to Cincinnati with my mind buzzing.

I had made the trip to the Super Museum hoping to gather information to dismantle Jean's delusional system, but ended up with enough information to consider dismantling my own hypotheses. I felt I had totally misperceived Jean's experience. What I had called an alter personality or a George Reeves archetype was now in question. Was Jean correct in her belief that George Reeves was with her? Was Jean *possessed* by George?

Jean

In the car tears flowed down my cheeks. George came through for me. Gary kept saying he was blown away and couldn't believe what had happened. Our conversation was so intense we missed our turnoff and it took us an extra ninety minutes to get home.

Gary, George, and I were very excited by the trip's success.

Through Jean, George verified this costume's authenticity and told Jim and Gary when George had last worn it.

PART II

Scientific Analyses and Spiritual Conclusions

Jean told her therapist, Gary Duncan, that her part of this story ended with her divorce from her then husband, Duncan Cline.

The rest of this story continues with Gary's analyses of the facts.

ΤΣΜ

Reevaluating the Twin Soul Concept

The nameless is the beginning of heaven and earth.
The named is the mother of ten thousand things.
—Tao Te Ching

Shortly after returning from Metropolis, I finished reading *Hollywood Kryptonite*. I discussed the Jean and George case in depth with Daryl in light of what I had witnessed at the Super Museum. It became evident that I needed to reexamine the phenomenon of twin souls, and assess the possibility of spirit possession with Jean.

I reevaluated Joudry's concept of twin souls and placed the phenomenon in a Jungian archetypal structure, which was a theoretical framework I was comfortable working with. From this perspective, the twin soul phenomenon could be understood as the archetypal constructs of anima and animus. These are archetypal patterns representing the male and female contra-sexual components of the personality. Men have feminine patterns that manifest as a female archetypal structure called the anima. Women have masculine patterns manifesting as the male archetype called the animus.

From a Jungian perspective, Jean and George are the contra-sexual components of a single soul. In this case, Jean would be the anima or female component of the soul's structure and George would be the animus, or male component. Together they formed the contra-sexual energetic dynamics of their complete soul.

Once Jean and George's intact soul split into two contra-sexual components, the two soul components were able to incarnate as individuated souls throughout many lifetimes. Individuated souls take on the appearance of being separate entities but, in fact, the appearance of separateness is an illusion.

According to Jean and George, the reason they split into two separate souls was to experience love from different perspectives in various lifetimes as male and female. Once they had incarnated through a variety of love relationships they would then merge back into a single intact soul.

I researched many religions and found that Spiritualists believe that twin souls are formed from spiritual energy. Spiritual energy separates into many soul fragments and these fragments form into separate souls and incarnate into many lifetimes.

Once these soul fragments incarnate into many lifetimes and learn what they need to learn, they then begin to merge back together and eventually all fragments merge into two penultimate fragments. These two soul fragments are considered twin souls and they eventually merge into a complete single soul. Once the soul is complete, it then moves into higher spiritual dimensions.

Both Joudry and the Spiritualists indicate that soul parts merge back together only after a period of lesson learning. On this point, George's explanation was somewhat different. He explained that twin souls experience many lifetimes until they remember their intended purpose; then they merge back together. From this perspective, the soul does not learn anything novel, but only remembers it true purpose.

Although I now understood twin souls from an archetypal perspective of anima and animus, I felt the phenomenon was somewhat limiting and did not address the larger picture regarding the true nature of the soul.

Based on my experience with archetypal patterns, I understood those patterns to be metaphors representing phenomena occurring on deeper levels of consciousness. I felt Jean and George were having a spiritual experience as twin souls but they did not understand the twin soul experience metaphorically. I believed the twin soul metaphor was Jean and George's myth pointing to a profound spiritual phenomenon.

I temporarily set aside the twin soul concept and considered the concept of possession. If George was really a discarnate spirit, then was this spirit possessing Jean?

I decided to contact Rob Tartz, a friend who lives in San Diego. Rob was also a friend and colleague of the noted consciousness researcher Stanley Krippner and their input on the phenomenon of possession would be a valuable asset to the case. Unlike Rob and Stanley, whose understanding of possession was primarily psychological, my experience with the topic was in the context of religion. During the 1980's and early 1990's I performed several spirit exorcisms under the direction of a priest in the Christian tradition. In these cases, the attached entities were malevolent and harmful to their hosts. Jean's experience with George appeared to be positive.

Rob suggested some books on the topic and, once I read them, I began using their descriptive criteria to assess Jean for possible possession.

I considered my observations of Jean's trance-like reactions. A true trance state would result in a temporary marked alteration in Jean's state of consciousness where she would lose her sense of personal identity when George's identity emerged. This did not occur when George was present. Rather, Jean maintained awareness of her identity as well as George's. When George was present, there was no constriction in Jean's awareness of herself or her external reality. She appeared to be psychologically present at all times.

Except for her masculine mannerisms when George was present, Jean displayed no unusual behaviors or movements, which would appear to be beyond her conscious control. During these periods, George did not replace Jean's sense of personal identity with his own. They were both able to communicate with each other as if they were two separate people and this occurred at all times. George did not control Jean in any discernable way.

At times, while George was present there were slight changes in Jean's facial and vocal expressions accompanying the masculine mannerisms, but not to the extent, her personal sense of identity was altered. Although, the vocal expressions were somewhat harsher in tone, it was still Jean's feminine voice. During these periods, Jean did not experience full or partial amnesia as in most cases of possession. I could access Jean or George at any time. If George did not wish to speak, either he or Jean would say so, but he was never inaccessible.

Jean and George's identities remained coherent. There was no indication Jean controlled George nor did George control Jean; they appeared to be two separate identities inhabiting one body. By definition, the spirit of George Reeves was not possessing Jean in any way.

After this reassessment period, and in light of Jean's display of intimate knowledge about George Reeves at the Super Museum, I began changing my clinical assessment of Jean. I no longer believed she was delusional. I no longer believed that George was an alter personality. I began to believe Jean's relationship with George was archetypal, a metaphor pointing to a deeper spiritual phenomenon.

I remained in a quandary over how Jean was able to manifest an image of George Reeves emanating from her body, which I had clearly witnessed a few weeks before the Metropolis trip. Because of this unusual manifestation, I knew I needed more information regarding the psychic substance, ectoplasm.

I wondered how Jean's overall perception of the Super Museum experience differed from mine. Throughout the trip she moved into several semi-trance states. I reasoned that, since Jean had experienced these events in an altered state, her perception would be markedly different than mine. Jean's perception of the events may give valuable clues into how she and George are sharing their perceptual awareness.

I obtained relevant information from Jean's diary on how she perceives situations. I also gained insight into how she experiences her emotional and physical changes. She was struggling with major internal changes and coming to terms with the fact she is sharing her body with a spirit who calls itself George Reeves. By sharing her body with this spirit, she is undergoing a profound physical transformation in which she is looking more like the actor George Reeves.

Since Jean's diary had been an asset in helping me understand relevant information regarding this case, I was looking forward to reading more of the uncensored ideas in the hope of finding more answers. However, my hopes of finding more information suddenly ended a week after her divorce. Jean gave me the last sections of the diary she was willing to contribute to the book project and informed me her part of the book ended with the divorce from Duncan. Although she continued to keep a diary, I was no longer privy to its contents.

As Jean is going through her emotional and physical transformation, I am undergoing major changes as well. Jean has presented me with a phenomenon that has challenged the very core of my belief system. I have witnessed that which is normally consigned to the fringes of reality. I have been forced to come to terms with the fact Jean is experiencing a most unusual phenomenon.

Understanding Psychic Connections

The difficulty with relationships is that they blur boundaries that are used to determine who we are.
—Anonymous

Over the past several months Jean has been experiencing a profound psychic and physical transformation. She has been connecting with me psychically in new ways. We often dream about the same people on the same nights. Jean often experiences my physical sensations even though she is not present and could not know when I am having them.

I thought Jean was probably picking up subtle cues from me, internalizing them, and later responding to them psycho-physiologically. However, Jean's psychic transformation took on new meaning for me in early spring. My chiropractor was conducting a heat treatment on my lower back to relieve kidney stone pain. I later learned Jean was feeling heat sensations on her lower back at the same time.

Weeks later, I had a radioactive dye test to locate where the stones were lodged. When the dye was injected into my left arm, I felt intense chills and the technician covered me with a blanket. I later discovered that Jean felt a cold sensation running up her left arm at the same time I was receiving the dye test.

These incidents made me realize the degree and intensity to which Jean was psychically experiencing my physical sensations.

During our second trip to the Super Museum, Daryl noticed that when Jim tested Jean, he stepped back, squinted, and asked, "What does 'Poppy' mean?" Then he quickly looked away.

Jean said George told her that he used to call his stepfather "Poppy." Jim looked frightened by this, which I found odd because George had answered much tougher questions during our last visit. Why was Jim acting so unusual? Upon further observation I noted, among other things, that Jim seldom looked at Jean, nor did he address questions directly to her, but rather through Daryl or me. I realized that Jim Hambrick was responding to Jean's physical transformation into the likeness of George Reeves. He was terrified by it. This made sense.

Daryl and I had witnessed this transformation slowly over time. Jim hadn't seen Jean in six months. Of course it would be shocking to him.

George's spirit co-existing in Jean's body, and sharing spiritual energies, was having a profound effect on Jean's total experience. This sharing of spiritual energy facilitated not only Jean's physical transformation, but her psychic abilities as well.

TΣM

I responded to a summons to appear in probate court because I was co-executor of a deceased client's estate. Since George had accompanied me in the past, I asked him to accompany me to the probate hearing. I felt that because Jean was looking more like George in appearance, their souls were more tightly integrated and had become significantly fused. I was curious if this fusion would prevent George from separating from her.

The day of the probate hearing, I looked around the courtroom and wondered if George was present. Shortly after the proceeding was underway the magistrate asked me a question. I stammered a second to collect my thoughts and then answered. The conclusions of the probate hearing went very well and lasted approximately two hours. I later learned, George was indeed present, which indicated although his and Jean's souls were integrated and fused, he could still separate from her at will.

Through Jean, George described the court scenes accurately. He disclosed how I stammered on the first question, gave details about the layout of the courtroom, and described how the two presiding attorneys were dressed. George described how the attorneys responded, demonstrated their handshakes, and gave an account of the verbal exchanges after the preceding was over.

I surmised that since George had forged a psychic link with me through our previous experiments, this link was transferred to Jean because they are sharing each other's spiritual energy. This unusual psychic linkage demonstrates that personality boundaries are merely an illusion, as is the boundary between life and death. Reality is a single, coherent manifestation.

Psychometric Analysis of Jean and George

We turn to using quantities when we can't compare the qualities ...
—Marvin Minsky

My colleague, Rob Tartz, indicated he was interested in interviewing Jean and George. Rob was interested in observing Jean's physical transformation and how Jean and George interacted. After the interview Jean and George told me that they liked Rob very much and were pleased he was consulting on the case.

When Rob and I got a chance to discuss the case in detail, he indicated Jean appeared to be mentally stable. He thought the interactions between Jean and George were quite interesting. He also indicated Jean's appearance was very masculine and she did have an uncanny resemblance to George Reeves. Rob and I concluded the conversation by agreeing that Jean and George sharing their sexual energies was a significant component to her physical transformation.

After further research, I found information relevant to Jean and George's sexual experience in Taoist literature. The Taoist discovered that life energy permeates all existence and they called this life energy chi. The Taoist also discovered that sexual energy is composed of a particular form of chi called ching chi. Ching chi is the sexual energy used in Taoist magickal practices to effect changes in the physical and spiritual world.

In Jean's case, this energy was transforming her physically to look like George Reeves, but I still did not understand how the process actually worked.

I felt confident that chi played a significant role in the shapeshifting process and decided to turn my attention to the past-life Jean, George, and I had supposedly lived in the Old South.

I found it somewhat disconcerting that Jean's past-life regressions indicated I had lived a lifetime with them in the Old South. In the mid 1980's, long before I had met Jean Cline, I had taken a course from the Edgar Cayce Foundation on how to discover our past lives. One of the four past-lives that surfaced as a result of this course was a lifetime I had lived in the Old South as a taskmaster in the slave fields.

During this past-life experience, intense feelings surfaced clustering around the fact I was poor and from a humble background. In the visual imagery component of my regression experience, I saw a white plantation house with a large porch. A slender-yet-domineering, bearded plantation owner dressed in white stood on the porch. I was on the steps looking up at him. I was dressed in a blue and white checkered shirt, brown pants, and brown muddy boots. I carried a whip and was the overseer of African American slaves working the cotton fields.

Jean's past-life regressions revealed nearly all of these same details, yet I was not to meet her in person for another decade.

I have always considered past-life scenarios to be metaphoric dramas being played out on a stage in our psyches. These dramas represent some current conflict, which appears to be occurring in another time and the characters playing the parts are archetypal figures pointing to a deeper phenomenon. Based on this perception I decided to explore the archetypal dynamics in Jean's personality. Since I had originally believed George Reeves was a hero archetype, the focus of my inquiry was to isolate other hero archetypes active in her personality.

The instrument I chose to identify these archetypal structures was the Heroic Myth Index, which determines the degree of activity of twelve standard hero archetypes active in all of us. Whether George Reeves was a spirit or not, the role he played throughout Jean's life was as a hero who rescued her from a conflicted childhood environment in which she felt abandoned.

Because of these abandonment issues, Jean created a fantasy world in which her hero George Reeves helped her cope with the death of her mother and rescued her from the drab conflict-ridden environment with her father. Based on this history, I hypothesized that the active hero archetypes present in Jean were probably the Orphan, the Innocence, and the Caregiver. The Orphan because she felt victimized and exploited; the Innocence, because she felt abandoned and in need of rescue; and the Caregiver, because of the domestic demands put on her by her father.

Heroic Myth Index

In late December, 1997, Jean took the Heroic Myth Index (Form E) and the results indicated her most active hero archetypes are: the Innocence, the Orphan, the Caregiver, the Destroyer, and the Magician. Although the scores indicated the Innocence and the Orphan archetypes were active, they were significantly less active than I had expected.

Because the Innocence and the Orphan hero archetypes were moderately low in activity, this most likely indicated the spirit of George Reeves had a significant influence on Jean's life. George had helped Jean deal with her exploitation and abandonment issues, which ordinarily would have been more pronounced in a case like Jean's. When George came to Jean when she was thirteen years old, she no longer felt abandoned and exploited, but felt loved and cared for. George helped Jean maintain a sense of safety and security.

Since Jean had been placed in the caregiver role early in her life, it was not surprising that the Caregiver hero archetype was highly active. The Caregiver hero archetype was strengthened over time by Jean's role as a practicing nurse.

The shadow side of the Caregiver archetype was also active, indicating the presence of codependent relationship patterns. A codependent relationship is one in which each partner unconsciously agrees to sabotage the relationship by setting up dysfunctional communication and behavior patterns. These patterns emerge from the ego defense mechanism *reaction formation,* which results from dysfunctional family relationships. Reaction formation is an unconscious dynamic in which repressed resentments are reorganized and then expressed as loving and caring behaviors.

Jean's father was a demanding and controlling personality and did not allow her to have a normal childhood. Jean became responsible for household duties and caring for her younger brother. She became her father's caretaker as well.

Emerging from this dysfunctional family environment, Jean began to harbor feelings of hurt, anger, and resentment. Because Jean was a "good girl," she could not consciously accept the negative feelings, so she repressed them. Once these negative feelings were securely repressed, Jean acted toward her father and brother with love, caring, and kindness. The reaction formation dynamic was in full operation.

Because of these dynamics, Jean appeared to be loving, caring, kind and friendly. She would go out of her way to help others to the detriment of herself. In essence, Jean became a pleaser, while subconsciously harboring feelings of hurt, anger, and resentment.

Jean was destined to experience dysfunctional relationships in her adulthood. She became codependent with her husband Duncan. She became Duncan's caretaker, which was the same role she had with her father.

Through our therapy sessions, Jean became aware of her co-dependence. She eventually realized she needed the strength to dissolve the relationship with Duncan, which would allow her to let go of the past and create the new life she so strongly desired for herself. Her strength came from the relationship she had with the spirit of George Reeves. George empowered Jean to make some drastic changes in her life, which activated the Destroyer hero archetype. This archetype usually emerges during major periods of growth and metamorphosis in which the individual needs to let go and start anew. In Jean's case, the Destroyer hero archetype became highly active because she began letting go of the past and started dissolving the codependent relationship with Duncan.

The Magician hero archetype was also active in Jean. The Magician hero archetype usually emerges during periods of great transformation, and with Jean, it was the most active of all the other archetypes. The high activity of this archetype reflects Jean's profound physical transformation into the likeness of George Reeves.

Personality Inventories

The results from the Heroic Myth Index were congruent with the information I had acquired on Jean's life. Based on these results, I became interested in further evaluating Jean's personality. I decided to incorporate three popular personality inventories: the Myers-Briggs, the MMPI, and the NEO PI-R. My primary interest was to ascertain if the results from these inventories would be congruent with the subjective personality assessments I had conducted earlier. I was not interested in assessing discrete personality variables, but obtaining an overview of Jean's personality as a whole.

Each inventory focuses on different dimensions of the personality. The Myers-Briggs ascertains personality type. This instrument indicates the types of personality preferences an individual has. These preferences are introversion (I) or extraversion (E), which is where an individual focuses his attention; intuition (N) or sensation (S) is the way an individual looks at things; thinking (T) or feeling (F) is the way an individual makes decisions about things; and judging (J) or perceiving (P), is how one deals with the outer world.

The MMPI, or Minnesota Multiphasic Personality Inventory, is an instrument that assesses various categories of psychopathology. The MMPI is normed on pathological populations and an individual taking this instrument is comparing their responses to the responses of those populations. If a preponderance of responses are the same as those given by a particular pathological population, then the test-taker may have similar pathologies.

The NEO PI-R or Revised NEO Personality Inventory is an instrument that assesses the personality in general. It is normed on non-pathological populations. This instrument assesses five personality domains: neuroticism, extraversion, openness, agreeableness, and conscientiousness.

George Lester, an outside clinical psychologist acquainted with the case, agreed to interpret both the MMPI and NEO PI-R. Dr. Lester indicated he would waive the fee if both Jean *and* the spirit George Reeves took the tests separately. These tests have built-in devices to check for answer consistency and faking. In other words, the test-taker cannot "cheat." Playing devil's advocate, Dr. Lester wondered whether George's scores would trip these built-in anti-faking devices.

I thought administering the inventories to both Jean and George separately was a novel idea, so I decided to do this with the Myers-Briggs as well. Jean and George agreed to take all three inventories separately. Testing began in mid October 1998 and spanned a three-week period with Jean and George taking the tests on separate days.

Myers-Briggs

Jean's Myers-Briggs results were at first confusing because her actual preference scores were an ISFP. However, Jean acted in the external world as an ISFJ personality type. Internally she is an ISFP and externally she acts as an ISFJ. Jean has an introversion preference indicating she focuses on her inner world; a sensing preference indicating she collects information about her world through her five senses; a feeling preference indicating she processes and makes decisions on information by the way she feels about it; and both a perceiving and a judging preference indicating she lives a highly structured lifestyle externally, but internally she does not like structure. The ISFP personality type is common for people in the nursing profession. Jean had been a nurse for three decades at the time of testing.

George's Myers-Briggs results indicated his personality type was ESFP. George has an extroversion preference indicating he focuses on the outer world; a sensing preference indicating he collects information about his world through the five senses; a feeling preference in which he processes and makes decisions on information by the way he feels about it; and a perceiving preference indicating he likes an unstructured spontaneous lifestyle. The ESFP personality type is congruent with individuals whose career choice is acting.

MMPI

A week after Jean and George took the Myers-Briggs, I administered the MMPI to each of them, again on separate days. The Myers-Briggs yielded two very different personality types for Jean and George. The personality preferences were congruent with their career choices and other personality traits. I was very impressed, but nevertheless wondered whether the MMPI—a more sophisticated instrument—would also yield two distinct personality profiles.

This time Dr. George Lester interpreted the results and checked the tests for validity. Dr. Lester verified that both MMPI profiles were valid, which meant Jean and George answered the questions truthfully. And once again, two different personality profiles emerged.

The majority of Jean's MMPI scores hovered around or below the normal range. There was nothing out of the ordinary or unexpected in her profile.

George's MMPI profile was very different from Jean's. All of George's scores were distributed well within normal range with the exception of an elevated sociopathic score. Based on information I obtained from *Hollywood Kryptonite,* and from interviews with Jim Hambrick and the spirit of George Reeves, the elevated sociopathic score was not surprising.

Whereas Jean used reaction formation to deal with her negative feelings, George used the ego defense mechanism *compensation* to deal with his mother's controlling and demanding nature. George compensated for Helen's controlling nature by creating a lifestyle for himself that was out of control.

This out of control lifestyle was a reaction against Helen's highly structured environment in which she told George what clothes to wear, whom to be friends with, and whom to date. As George grew older, he began to rebel and take control of his life. His first act of defiance against Helen was he became a boxer, which infuriated her because she could do nothing about it. He continued to compensate by moving further into a spontaneous, uncontrolled, and unstructured lifestyle. These self-destructive patterns moved him in a sociopathic direction.

George became more sociopathic as he began to drink heavily and take more risks with his life. He became a gambler and a party boy. He even played the "game," pointing an unloaded gun at his head and pulling the trigger.

NEO PI-R

Dr. George Lester verified and interpreted the NEO PI-R test results. The pattern was familiar as yet again two distinct personality profiles had emerged.

Jean's NEO PI-R neuroticism scores indicated the presence of anxiety, anger, apprehensiveness, shyness, sadness, loneliness, and self-consciousness.

Her extraversion scores indicated she was a loner, preferred a slow steady pace to life, and did not enjoy large crowds.

The openness scores indicated the presence of an active fantasy life, love of the arts and music, a strong connection with her feelings and emotions, a low need for variety in her life, and open-mindedness.

Jean's agreeableness scores indicated she is not trusting of others, somewhat guarded in expressing feelings, willingness to help others in need, has low self-esteem, and puts the needs and interests of others before her own.

The conscientiousness scores indicated Jean was somewhat neat and tidy, well organized, self-disciplined, dependable and cautious, but did not feel prepared to deal with life.

Jean's NEO PI-R profile was congruent with the findings of the Myers-Briggs, which indicated Jean was introverted. The NEO PI-R indicated Jean puts the needs and interest of others before her own. This result supports the presence of the highly active Caregiver hero archetype.

George's NEO PI-R scores were very different from Jean's. His neuroticism scores indicated he does not worry, is slow to anger, and is cheerful, not prone to guilt, not shy, apprehensive or easily embarrassed, and has poor control over impulses and desires.

The extraversion scores indicated George is warm and affectionate, enjoys large noisy crowds and the company of others, speaks without hesitation, has leadership qualities and high energy levels, enjoys excitement, stimulation and thrills, can laugh easily, and is optimistic.

The openness scores indicated George has a good imagination, loves the arts and music, is open about his feelings, has a need for variety in his life, is open-minded to new ideas, and has the ability to reexamine traditional values.

The agreeableness scores indicated George is trusting and believes in others, is straightforward and frank, has a willingness to assist and help others in need, easily forgives and forgets, is somewhat humble, and has sympathy and concern for others.

The conscientiousness scores indicated George feels somewhat prepared to deal with life, is somewhat organized, dependable and reliable, has high aspirations for work and career, has low self-discipline and self-control, and can be somewhat hasty and act without thinking things through.

George's NEO PI-R profile was congruent with the Myers-Briggs indicating that he was an extrovert. In addition, the NEO PI-R profile indicated George had a need for variety in his life, was somewhat organized and had low self-discipline. These results support the Myers-Briggs perceiving preference in which George likes a spontaneous and unstructured lifestyle. The NEO PI-R results also indicated George was not prone to guilt, had poor control over impulses and desires, enjoyed excitement, stimulation and thrills, had low self-discipline, low self-control and could be somewhat hasty and act without thinking things through, which supports the MMPI's elevated sociopathic score.

TΣM

The results of the Myers-Brigs, the MMPI, and the NEO PI-R indicate that there appears to be two distinct identities existing in Jean. These three inventories are congruent with the known histories of Jean Cline and George Reeves and the subjective evaluations I conducted earlier.

Jean's and George's Myers-Briggs personality test results showing the emergence of two distinct personality profiles.

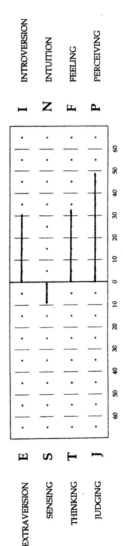

Report Form for the Myers-Briggs Type Indicator®

Name: George B. Reeves

Sex: ☑ Male ☐ Female   Date: 10/14/98

The MBTI™ reports your preferences on four scales. There are two opposite preferences on each scale. The four scales deal with where you like to focus your attention (E or I), the way you like to look at things (S or N), the way you like to go about deciding things (T or F), and how you deal with the outer world (J or P). Short descriptions of each scale are shown below.

E	You prefer to focus on the outer world of people and things	or **I**	You prefer to focus on the inner world of ideas and impressions
S	You tend to focus on the present and on concrete information gained from your senses	or **N**	You tend to focus on the future, with a view toward patterns and possibilities
T	You tend to base your decisions on logic and on objective analysis of cause and effect	or **F**	You tend to base your decisions primarily on values and on subjective evaluation of person-centered concerns
J	You like a planned and organized approach to life and prefer to have things settled	or **P**	You like a flexible and spontaneous approach to life and prefer to keep your options open

REPORTED TYPE: | E | S | F | P |

PREFERENCE SCORES: | 3 | 3 | 17 | 13 |

The four letters show your Reported Type, which is the combination of the four preferences you chose. There are sixteen possible types.

Preference scores show how consistently you chose one preference over the other; high scores usually mean a clear preference. Preference scores do *not* measure abilities or development.

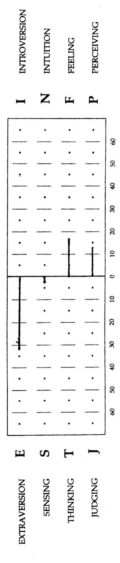

EXTRAVERSION	E		I	INTROVERSION
SENSING	S		N	INTUITION
THINKING	T		F	FEELING
JUDGING	J		P	PERCEIVING

Each type tends to have different interests and different values. On the back of this page are very brief descriptions of each of the sixteen types. Find the one that matches the four letters of your Reported Type and see whether it fits you. If it doesn't, try to find one that does. For a more complete description of the types and the implications for career choice, relationships, and work behavior, see *Introduction to Type* by Isabel Briggs Myers. Remember that everyone uses each of the preferences at different times; your Reported Type shows which you are likely to prefer the most and probably use most often.

 Consulting Psychologists Press, Inc.
577 College Avenue, Palo Alto, California 94306

Copyright © 1976 by Isabel Briggs Myers. Copyright © 1988 by Consulting Psychologists Press. All rights reserved. Reproduction of either side of this form by any process is unlawful without the Publisher's written permission. MBTI is a trademark and Myers-Briggs Type Indicator is a registered trademark of Consulting Psychologists Press, Inc.

TΣM

Metaphysical Explanation of Shapeshifting

What we shall find is an exemplification, an encouragement, and a refinement of old wisdom.
—J. Robert Oppenheimer

After months of diligent therapeutic work, Jean was finally adjusting to the fact she was physically changing into the appearance of George Reeves. Once the adjustment was somewhat secure, George began stressing that they should go public with their experience. George wanted the public to know that he and Jean were twin souls and her physical transformation was the result of their two souls merging. Their soul merger also indicated this was their last love incarnation on the physical plane. As twin souls, Jean and George have experienced a variety of love relationships throughout many incarnations. They have loved as husband and wife, brother and sister, and in this lifetime they have loved as spirit and mortal.

At first, Jean was reluctant to go public but George convinced her there was nothing to worry about. He stressed he would assist her the same way he did at the Super Museum with all the relevant details she needed about his earthly life. All Jean had to do was to stay calm and not block his communication.

I thought going public would be an excellent opportunity to gauge people's reactions to Jean's profound physical transformation. From November 1998 to September 1999, Jean, Daryl, and I made several public appearances. We lectured locally at various groups, including the Noetic Science Institute, the Near Death Study group, and the Theosophical Society. We had appearances at metaphysical bookstores, New Age expos, community groups, psychic festivals, and women's groups. We even had two television interviews.

I became fascinated with how people responded to the Jean and George phenomenon. Some people said they could see the appearance of George Reeves in Jean; some said it became more pronounced when he spoke through her. Some people didn't focus on Jean's appearance at all, but instead discussed their personal twin soul experiences. There were women who felt George was possessing Jean and should be exorcised. One woman even claimed George was an evil spirit!

These reactions to Jean's physical transformation indicated that many people besides Daryl and I could see the likeness of George Reeves manifesting in Jean. Although I was witnessing this profound physical transformation, and even knew that chi energy was a critical component, I still felt unable to adequately explain how the process worked.

Finally, in the autumn of 2000, I found the key that unlocked the secret to Jean's physical transformation. I was browsing through a large bookstore when I came across an interesting book on shapeshifting by Rosalyn Greene. This was the first work that presented in detail how the shapeshifting process occurred.

I was amazed to discover that the shapeshifting phenomena took several forms, which included mental shifting, astral shifting, possession shifting, apparition shifting, bilocation shifting and the rarest form, was physical shifting. The two types of shapeshifting applicable to Jean's experience were mental shifting and physical shifting.

On a macro level, Greene detailed the steps on how a human shapeshifts into animal form. The first step is for the individual to cultivate the animal he or she desires to become, and then create a mental bond with that animal. Step two is to meditate to raise chi energy to the highest level possible.

Chi or life energy is the energy of the soul that animates all living organisms and has been referred to by many names, such as huna, ka, orgone, ki, prana, nous, animal magnetism, and Holy Spirit. Chi is the energy source that not only animates all life but also facilitates the shapeshifting or physical transformation process.

In the third step, the shifter refocuses attention on finding the desired archetypal animal that resides deep within the collective unconscious. Once the archetypal animal is located, the shifter moves into the fourth step, using mental imagery to focus chi energy into the archetypal animal. Finally, the shifter begins to act and think like the archetypal animal. Once these steps have been successfully performed over an extended period, which could take several years, the shifter then begins to shift mentally into the archetypal animal.

Once the shifter can mentally shift into the desired animal, the next step is physical shifting. In this step, the shifter finds the desired animal's habitat, then visits and explores the surroundings, experiencing the area as the animal would.

While in the habitat, the shifter again raises chi energy to the highest level possible and experiences the fullness of the energy to the point where it can no longer be contained. Then the shifter moves into the desired animal posture, focusing and integrating chi energy into the archetypal animal. Once integrated, the shifter lets go of control and allows chi to facilitate the shapeshifting process.

The shifter's senses and food interests become like the animal's. Hair growth may appear on the stomach area, hands, or feet, as appropriate. The nose may elongate into a snout, depending on the archetypal animal, and eventually the human body becomes indistinguishable from the authentic animal form. This physical transformation lasts for a short period and then the individual transforms back into human form.

It can take many years of diligent inner work for an individual to cultivate the animal psyche that allows physical shifting to occur. Rosalyn Greene indicated she has not cultivated the technique of physical shifting but since childhood, she has been a mental shifter, which is the most common type. Being a mental shifter has given Greene access into the shadow world of shapeshifting. Greene has interviewed physical shifters and people who have witnessed the physical shapeshifting in process.

Greene's metaphysical model of shapeshifting was specific to how humans shift into animal form, but did not address how humans physically transform into another human form. With some additional research, however, I was able to rework Greene's metaphysical model of shapeshifting to explain how humans could shift into another human form.

I applied this newfound knowledge to Jean's unusual experience. For the first time since taking on this case, I felt I had a framework that could explain how Jean was transforming into the likeness of George Reeves. This framework also explained the ectoplasmic manifestation of George Reeves that emerged from Jean's face about a week before we took our first trip to the Super Museum.

Spiritual Conclusions

Spiritual truth is a truth of the spirit, not a truth of the intellect, not a mathematical theorem or a logical formula.
—Sri Aurobindo

Carolyn Shilt , the Dayton, Ohio psychic Daryl had visited in 1994, predicted our entire experience two years before it began. When Daryl and I realized Carolyn's prediction had materialized, we were both stunned. We realized the only way she could have made such an accurate prediction, was that the experience with Jean and George had already existed on the spiritual level. As a psychic, Carolyn had only tapped into the twin soul energy that was already there.

When analyzed from this perspective it's clear that the concept of twin souls has a deeper meaning than we'd first realized. Twin souls are two parts of a complete soul that split into its male and female components forming a duality. As male and female, Jean and George could experience this physical reality, which can only sustain its existence as duality. Once a duality on the physical plane merges, the energy is sent back to the spiritual plane, to God.

Although, Jean and George are twin souls they are still two parts of one soul and that soul is a part of a greater soul, which George calls "God." The twin soul is a metaphor for the illusion of dualities, which exist within the God experience. George says that although we appear to be separate, we are all one. We are all connected to each other.

It was clear from George's explanation everything that exists is a part of God. We individuals and all the universe, its dimensions, realities, and incarnations, exist within God. Everything is occurring in the eternal now. In other words, the human concept of time is an illusion.

What we perceive as past-lives are experiences our souls are concurrently having in parallel realities. When I regressed Jean to a past-life she lived with George in the Old South, what occurred in that experience was a shift in her conscious awareness to a parallel lifetime her soul was living alongside her current lifetime, all happening within the eternal now!

Jean had no conscious memory of the many lifetimes she had lived with George until I regressed her. The regressions shifted Jean's conscious awareness to those lifetimes. After the regressions Jean continued to remember minute details from those past-lives.

According to Jean and George, they chose to experience love in a variety of situations throughout many incarnations and in this lifetime their love is experienced as mortal and spirit. Because Jean is mortal and George is spirit, their love crosses the boundary between the physical world and spirit world, demonstrating that this boundary is an illusion. Upon Jean's death, she and George will merge back into the One, only to reemerge again as new separate souls having new experiences. George explained that love is the energy that binds and holds all souls together. This collective soul, held together by love, is God.

God *is* love.

George's Four Spiritual Messages

The unique experience of a mortal having a love relationship with a spirit has profound spiritual implications. The Jean and George phenomenon appears to be a unique manifestation occurring at a time when the world is moving into a major consciousness shift. Indeed, George has left us with four spiritual messages.

These spiritual messages are not new, but are part of the philosophical foundation of the world's great religions and spiritual disciplines. George reminds us of these messages, which could have a profound impact on our spiritual awareness if internalized and acted upon with conscious intention.

"We are all one; duality or separateness is an illusion."

The first message is we are all one; duality or separateness is an illusion. Not only are we all one with each other, but we are all one with everything. Jean and George's soul merger represents duality merging into oneness.

"Love is the binding energy that holds everything together."

The second message is that love is the binding energy that holds everything together. Love binds all souls together in all dimensions, realities, and lifetimes. Love binds together everything, keeping everything in harmony and balance within the God experience.

"All souls are free to choose any experience they desire."

The third message is all souls are free to choose any experience they desire. In other words, souls can create their own reality, allowing God to experience itself in many wondrous and innovative ways.

"Life is eternal and death is an illusion."

The fourth message is life is eternal, all souls are immortal and death is an illusion. When the soul leaves the physical body it continues to create new experiences in new incarnations as it journeys toward union with the oneness. Our souls never die. God is eternal and we are of God. Therefore we are eternal.

These four messages point the way to our future evolution as spiritual beings. This case has shown us a foundation upon which to alter our destiny in positive way. We gain a spiritual awareness of who we are and how we relate to each other. Ultimately, we see how we fit into God's grand experience.

TΣM

Epilogue

Whether we know it or not, we are all on a journey beyond belief...
—Roger Walsh

This case has allowed me to integrate two areas of my life that always seemed separate: the scientific and the spiritual. I've had a profound shift in perspective and now see reality as an undivided whole. This new perspective opened vast horizons in my spiritual awareness, which set the stage for a radical change in my life's direction.

As a psychotherapist, I felt constricted, limited, and burned out. I could no longer continue on that career path. My soul was leading me in a different direction. I realized I was no longer reading about psychotherapy, but voraciously consuming information on spirituality, the esoteric, and the mystical.

I began wondering why my soul was leading me in this spiritual direction. I decided if this was my true calling, I would immerse myself back into seminary studies. It wasn't long before I was ordained to the deaconate of the Gnostic Catholic Apostolic Autocephalous Church of North America. This ultimately led to the completion of my thesis on the Licentiate of Divine Letters in Theology and to my final ordination into the Gnostic priesthood.

Within a year, I completely dissolved my private psychotherapy practice. Daryl became a nutritional supplement sales representative and sold his vitamin business. We then began a new adventure, moving from Cincinnati to North Carolina, which was part of Daryl's sales territory.

Once settled, I created two courses I had been interested in teaching for sometime: a course in Critical Thinking and a course on the parallel sayings of Buddha and Christ. I contacted several local colleges and asked whether they'd be interested in having me teach these courses. None of the colleges were interested in the Critical Thinking course, but Duke University was interested in the parallel sayings of Buddha and Christ. By autumn 2004, I was teaching the course.

The course got off to a good start but I soon noticed the students asked many questions about western esoteric and mystical traditions. I also discovered the students knew more about the eastern religions than they knew about their own traditions. They were starved to learn more about their own western inner traditions and I had studied these for over thirty-five years. By the end of autumn term, I finally knew where my soul was leading me. I was destined to lecture on the western esoteric, mystical, and spiritual traditions.

TΣM

Jean's life had changed forever. She would never again be the person who married George Owens or Duncan Cline. Over the next few years, I had little contact with Jean. However, through Daryl, I knew she had found a position with Children's Hospital in Cincinnati as a home health nurse. It wasn't until I started converting my clinical notes and her diary into a narrative that Jean and I began communicating consistently twice a month.

I knew Jean's physical transformation was continuing because she told me people sometimes called her "sir" or "mister."

TΣM

It was during this period Daryl began reviewing the influences that had shaped his life. His grandmother, Carrie Coston, who raised Daryl, was a very religious woman. She exposed Daryl to healings, speaking in tongues, and other mystical experiences. These early experiences laid the groundwork for his interest in all aspects of spirituality.

In the late 1980's, while pursuing a degree in psychology, Daryl became part of a team that investigated hauntings and other paranormal phenomena. His encounters with people who experienced the paranormal soon lead him to the psychic, Carolyn Shilt, who foretold of the Jean and George experience. Daryl's involvement in the Jean and George case continued to shape his spirituality. Then in the summer of 1997, he discovered Neil Donald Walsch's *Conversations with God* series, which helped him integrate the various aspect of his spirituality.

Daryl's ability to articulate spiritual insights helped shape the final chapters of this book. Daryl's insights helped shape the spiritual implications of the Jean and George phenomenon into a coherent assessment.

With all the assessments and investigations Daryl and I have conducted on this case, we have come to believe the evidence supports the spirit present with Jean Cline is that of George Reeves. This does not negate the fact others may perceive the experience differently because we can't definitively verify that the spirit who calls itself George Reeves is really the late actor. I, however, know that I undertook this case with pure skepticism, and today I do believe the spirit with Jean is that of the late Superman actor, George Reeves. If George had to perform in order to convince this one-time skeptic, then it has indeed been an academy award performance.

PART III

Appendices, Glossary, and References

TΣM

Appendix A

Poem sent to Jack Larson on birthday anniversary 1997.

JACK'S POEM

Friends we were, the kid and me in early days upon TV.
We laughed and joked to pass the time,
And played the game.
And learned the lines.

There never was a lot to know,
The days and years just seemed to flow.
But one dark day it all would end,
Because the game was not pretend.

Now years have passed and you have thought
About those gone who meant a lot.
And wonder where we all can be, and is there
More than what we see?
What part is this that I can play?
Just like the kid in early days, a friend
Just as we were before.
Just ask and I will tell you more.

Of life and love that does not end,
The kid and I are friends again.
Remember Jack, I know you do,
Of those who really cared for you.

Look at her face and you will see
That she is quite a lot like me.
I'll tell you true just like before
Just what my life was really for.

A Psychological & Spiritual Journey

Appendix B

Parallels in the lives of George Reeves and Jean Cline

GEORGE   JEAN

BIRTH
Born in Northern Midwest   Born in Northern Midwest
(Iowa)   (Illinois)

PARENTAGE
Single parent (Mother)   Single parent (Father)
Parent directed career choice   Parent directed career choice

EDUCATION
Junior College   Junior College

PROFESSION
Public career, show business   Public career, nursing
Ended career working w/children   Ending career working w/children

GEORGE ##JEAN

PHYSICAL CHARACTERISTICS

Height six foot	Height six foot
Dark hair	Dark hair
Dark eyes	Dark eyes
Widow's peak	Widow's peak
Athletic build	Athletic build
Tenor voice	Tenor voice
Needed glasses early 40's	Needed glasses early 40's
Brown frame glasses	Brown frame glasses
Broke foot fencing	Broke foot tree climbing
Lacerated face in auto accident	Lacerated face in a fall

PERSONALITY

Generous and very sociable	Generous and very sociable

MARITAL

Married at age 25	Married at age 25

RELIGION

Member of high church (Catholic)	Member of high church (Episcopalian)

A Psychological & Spiritual Journey

GEORGE   JEAN

HOME

George	Jean
Enjoyed natural surrounding	Enjoyed natural surrounding
Bought Cape Cod type home	Bought Cape Cod type home
House backed up to hill location	House backed up to hill location

MISCELLANEOUS

George	Jean
Good horseman	Good horseman
Played string instrument (guitar)	Played string instrument (viola & Cello)
Claustrophobic	Claustrophobic
Had Cincinnati connections	Had Cincinnati connections
Suffer from wool allergy	Suffer from wool allergy

LAST YEARS OF LIFE

George	Jean
Job dissatisfaction	Job dissatisfaction
Considering career change	Considering career change
Auto accident near home after 45th birthday	Auto accident near home after 45th birthday

TΣM

Appendix C

Super Museum Challenge

The following is a compilation of the items that Jean successfully identified during trips to Jim Hambrick's Super Museum in Metropolis, Illinois. The trips took place on November 2nd and 3rd, 1996, and April 11th and 12th, 1997.

Jim Hambrick, curator of the museum and an expert on Superman and the life of George Reeves, verified virtually everything that Jean had told Gary during therapy sessions. However, the following list only highlights specific challenges posed to Jean in an effort to discern whether the spirit of George Reeves was able to answer questions through her.

1. Jean stated that George told her the Superman costume on display there was a facsimile. Mr. Hambrick verified this, stating the costume had been switched for insurance purposes, and only he and his insurance agent knew about this.

2. Jean correctly identified hundreds of photos of George's friends and family, even when such photos were wide-angle shots, group shots, and/or depicted such friends and family in the early years of their lives. These people included, of course, Toni Mannix and Helen Bessolo, but also obscure people, such as a cinematographer from the Superman series, and countless others.

3. Jean was able to pick out photos of George's home and changes that had been made since he lived there. Many rooms had been described to Gary Duncan in therapy months before the Super Museum visit. Jean was able to say when and where each photo was taken.

4. When asked, George instantly gave the age of Gene LaBell, his personal trainer at the time of George's death.

5. Jim brought out a test for Jean and she immediately identified a commemorative certificate from Pope Pius XII, with whom George had had an audience, during which he received the certificate. We tried to throw Jean off by asking, "Where did George hang the certificate?" Jean replied, "It wasn't hung. It was displayed on my dresser. Where's the cross that goes with it?" At the time Jim did not know about the cross, but during our second visit Jim told us that he'd since learned that Jean had indeed been correct, and that George used to keep a cross with the certificate.

6. Jean verified that George stayed with grandparents in Ashland, Kentucky before moving to Pasadena as a young child.

7. Through Jean, George discussed in detail the "flying" mechanism from the Superman series and how it worked. This had been previously described to Gary Duncan in therapy. Jim confirmed the description.

8. Verified relationship with Paulette Goddard.

9. Correctly answered a test question by Jim Hambrick about a secret game George and Jack Larson played on the set of Superman.

10. Verified that George, Phyllis Coates, and Noel Neill were only good friends; that there was no deeper relation with either of them.

11. Jim brought Jean and George another test: two costumes. Jean correctly stated the date each costume was used for the production of *The Adventures of Superman.*

12. Through Jean, George explained how Toni had placed printed wallpaper on the ceiling in the den.

13. Jean described a hill behind George's home and the fact that there were no windows in George's bedroom when he lived there.

14. When asked about the material in one of the costumes, George said the reason for it was due to an allergic reaction he had to wool.

15. Jean successfully answered another challenge question on April 12, 1997. When asked who Poppy was, she correctly answered Frank Bessolo, George's stepfather.

TΣM

Glossary

Alter personality: A secondary personality or personalities, which split off from the dominant core personality. These personalities can become autonomous with their own personal life histories.

Archetype: A primordial image manifesting as symbolic patterns, which emerges from the collective unconscious and can appear in many forms.

Chakra: Energetic centers that spin in the shape of vortexes and are distributed throughout the subtle energy bodies. The physical body has seven major chakras aligned along the spinal column and numerous minor chakras distributed throughout all the subtle bodies. The seven major chakras are connected to the nerve ganglia, cellular structure and the major glands allowing chi to energize the autonomic nervous system.

Codependent: An unconscious destructive mutual bond created between significant partners in a relationship. The relationship partners unconsciously help sustain pathological communication and behavioral patterns that sabotage the relationship as a whole and each partner individually.

Contrasexual: The male and female opposites that exist in the personality structure.

Delusions: False beliefs not grounded in objective or consensus reality.

Dissociation: Experiences that appear to exist apart from or disconnected from the main coherent flow of conscious awareness.

Dissociative Identity Disorder: The present of two or more distinct identities or personalities that recurrently takes controls of the core personality.

Ectoplasm: A living energetic exteriorized substance that emerges from the spiritual subtle bodies and is shaped by conscious or unconscious intentions.

Esoteric: The secret, mysterious, occult or hidden teachings, which are revealed to initiates of a sacred, religious, mystical, magickal groups or orders; commonly referred to as the inner mysteries or inner traditions.

Gnostic: An early form of Christianity that believed in attaining a special spiritual knowledge through the direct connection with the divine.

Hallucinations: False sensory perceptions that occur in the absence of corresponding external stimuli.

Hermeticism: A philosophy that emerged circa 15th century CE and refers in a broader sense to doctrines, beliefs and practices in western esotericism, Kabbalah, magick, alchemy and astrology.

Hypertrichosis: A genetic disorder in which hair is distributed over the entire body giving the appearance of a werewolf.

Imagery: Using the sense modalities to create an internal imaginative story or fantasy.

Kabbalah: The Jewish mystical system.

Lycanthropy: A mental disorder in which a person believes he is a werewolf.

Meditation: A variety of methods and techniques that brings consciousness into the here and now or present moment.

MMPI: A psychological test or inventory to detect the presence of psychopathology.

NEO PI-R: A personality test or inventory that assesses the general personality structure.

Myers-Briggs: A psychological test that detects personality preferences.

Mystical: The direct immediate experience with the Absolute or God or ultimate reality.

Past-Life Regression: One of several altered state of consciousness techniques that alters an individual's conscious awareness, resulting in the individual perceiving himself or herself experiencing a previous lifetime in which they lived.

Porphyria: A genetic disorder in which an individual lacks the pigment heme that carries oxygen in red blood cells.

Psychosis: A severe form of mental illness.

Psychometric: Pertaining to psychometrics, which is the branch of psychology that deals with the design, administration, and interpretation of quantitative tests for the measurement of psychological variables such as intelligence, aptitude, and personality traits.

Shapeshifting: The process of mentally, astrally and physically shifting into an animal or another human form.

Soul Family: A group of souls who have experienced many lifetimes together as a close net group, but do not have the close intimate relationship of soul mates.

Soul Mate: Souls who have experienced many lifetimes together in a one-on-one close intimate relationship, but are not two parts of the same soul as with twin souls.

Soul Merger: The spiritual phenomenon of two perceived separate souls merging back into a single soul.

Spirituality: The whole of inner experience in which one seeks connectedness with the divine, resulting in personal inner change and transformation through the use of prayer, contemplation, meditation or other spiritual practices.

Synchronistic: Pertaining to events that do not always obey the rules of time, space, and causality. These events are meaningful but not causally related; they link the psychic world to the material world.

Transpersonal: Refers to those aspects of the human experience concerned with reaching the highest potential, realization of unitive knowing and transcendent states of consciousness.

Twin Soul: The phenomenon in which a perceived single soul decides to separate into two individual souls to have a particular experience.

Bibliography

American Psychiatric Association. (1994). <u>Diagnostic and Statistical Manual of Mental Disorders (4th. ed.).</u> Washington, DC.

Asaad, G. (1990). <u>Hallucinations in Clinical Psychiatry.</u> New York: Brunner/Mazel.

Auerbach, L. (1996). <u>Mind over Matter.</u> New York: Kensington.

Austin. J. (1991). <u>Hollywood's Unsolved Mysteries.</u> New York: Wings. pp. 250-261.

Barber, P. (1988). <u>Vampires, Burial, and Death.</u> New Haven: Yale University.

Beahrs, J. O. (1982). <u>Unity and Multiplicity.</u> New York: Brunner/Mazel.

Bendit, L. J. & Bendit, P. D. (1989). <u>The Etheric Body of Man.</u> Wheaton: Theosophical.

Berger A.S. & Berger J. (1991). <u>The Encyclopedia of Parapsychology and Psychical Research.</u> New York: Paragon.

Berger, J. & Berger, A. (1991). <u>Reincarnation Fact or Fable.</u> London: Aquarian.

Bletzer, J. G. (1987). <u>Encyclopedic Psychic Dictionary.</u> Norfolk: Donning.

Bloch, J. P. (1991). <u>Assessment and Treatment of Multiple Personality and Dissociative Disorders.</u> Sarasota: Professional Resource.

Bottinelli, C. & Weidner, W. (1997, video). <u>Wolfman: Myth & the Science.</u>

Bourguignon. E. (1976). Possession. Prospect Heights: Waveland.

Brennan, J. H. (1990). Understanding Reincarnation. Glasgow: Aquarian.

Brothers, Everly. (1960). Let It Be Me. (Gilbert Bécaud, Mann Curtis, Pierre Delanoé).

Brussat, M. A. & Brussat, F. (Eds.). (1997). 100 More Ways to Keep Your Soul Alive. San Francisco: Harper.

Castaneda, C. (1968). The Teaching of Don Juan. Berkeley: University Of California.

Castaneda, C. (1987). The Power of Silence: Further Lessons of Don Juan. New York: Washington Square.

Castaneda, C. (1991). A Separate Reality: Further Conversations with Don Juan. New York: Washington Square.

Chadwick, G. (1988). Discovering Your Past Lives. New York: Contemporary.

Chia, M. & Winn, M. (1984). Taoist Secrets of Love: Cultivating Male Sexual Energy. Santa Fe: Aurora.

Crabtree, A. (1985). Multiple Man: In Possession and Multiple Personality. New York: Praeger.

Darion, J. & Leigh, M. (1965). The Impossible Dream. Man of La Mancha. Port Chester: Cherry Lane Music.

Darin, Bobby. (March 5, 1959). Dream Lover. Atco Records.

Davidoff, H. (Eds.). (1952). The Pocket Book of Quotations. New York: Pocket.

Davis, M & Lane, E. (1978). Rainbow of Life. New York: Harper.

De Guaita, S. (2004). The Mysteries of Solitude. L'Initiation, 4 (2), pp. 1-29.

Doore, G. (Eds.). (1990). What Survives? Los Angeles: Jeremy P. Tarcher.

Dunn-Mascett, M. (1992). Vampire. London: Viking Studio.

Evans, H. (1989). Alternate States of Consciousness. Northamptonshire: Aquarian.

Feather, K. E. (1995). A Toltec Path. Norfolk: Hampton Roads.

Ferguson, S. B. & Wright, D. F. (1988). New Dictionary of Theology. Downers Grove: InterVarsity.

Gooch, S. (1984). Creatures from Inner Space. London: Rider.

Goswami, A. (1993). The Self-Aware Universe. New York: Jeremy P. Tarcher/Putnam.

Greene, R. (2000). The Magic of Shapeshifting. York Beach: Samuel Weiser.

Gris H. & Dick, W. (1978). The New Soviet Psychic Discoveries. New York: Warner.

Grof, C. & Grof, S. (1989). Spiritual Emergency. Los Angeles: Jeremy P. Tarcher.

Grof, C. & Grof, S. (1990). The Stormy Search for the Self. New York: Jeremy P. Tarcher/Perigee.

Grossman, G. (1976). Serial to Cereal. New York: Popular Library.

Guiley, R. E. (1991). Encyclopedia of Mystical & Paranormal Experience. San Francisco: Harper.

Harrison, T. (1994). Stigmata: A Medieval Phenomenon in a Modern Age. New York: St. Martin's.

Head, J. & Cranston, S. (1979). Reincarnation: The Phoenix Fire Mystery. San Diego: Point Loma.

Henry, L. C. (Eds.). (1945). Five Thousand Quotations for All Occasions. New York: Doubleday.

Hilgard, E. R. (1977). Divided Consciousness. New York: John Wiley.

Hope, J. (1997). The Secret Language of the Soul. San Francisco: Chronicle

Inglis, Brian. (1989). Trance. London: Grafton.

Irwin, H. J. (1994). An Introduction to Parapsychology. Jefferson: McFarland.

Jamal, M. (1987). Shape Shifters. London: Arkana.

Joudry, P. & Pressman, M. (1995). Twin Souls. New York: Carol Southern.

Judith, A. (2004, Revised). Eastern Body, Western Mind: Psychology and the Chakra System as a Path to the Self. Berkeley: Celestial Arts.

Kashner, S. & Schoenberger, N. (1996). Hollywood Kryptonite. New York: St. Martin's.

Kluckhorn, C. (1944). Navaho Witchcraft. Boston: Beacon.

Konstantinos. (1996). Vampire the Occult Truth. St. Paul: Llewellyn

Krippner, S. & Rubin, D. (Eds.). (1974). The Kirlian Aura. New York: Doubleday/Anchor.

Krippner, S. & Powers, S. M. (1997). Broken Images, Broken Selves. Washington: Brunner/Mazel.

Leadbeater, C. W. (1978). The Inner Life. Wheaton: Theosophical.

Levy, H. S. & Ishihara, A. (1989). The Tao of Sex. Lower Lake: Integral.

Maurey, E. (1988). Exorcism. West Chester: Whitford.

Mc Kuen, R. (1967). Listen To The Warm. New York: Random House.

Millman, D. (1984). Way of the Peaceful Warrior. Berkeley: H. J. Kramer.

Mishlove, J. (1975). The Roots of Consciousness. New York: Random House.

Mishlove, J. (1983). PSI Development Systems. New York: Ballantine.

Monroe, R. A. (1994). Ultimate Journey. New York: Doubleday.

Newton, M. (1996). Journey of Souls. St. Paul: Llewellyn P.

Noll, R. (1992). Vampires, Werewolves, and Demons. New York: Brunner/Mazel.

Novak, P. (1997). The Division of Consciousness. Charlottesville: Hampton Roads.

O'Leary, B. (1989). Exploring Inner and Outer Space. Berkeley: North Atlantic.

Opie, I. & Tatem, M. (1990). A Dictionary of Superstitions. New York: Oxford University.

Ostrander, S. & Schroeder, L. (1971). Psychic Discoveries behind the Iron Curtain. New York: Bantam.

Ostrander, S. & Schroeder, L. (1974). Handbook of Psychic Discoveries. New York: Berkley Medallion.

Pearson, C.S (1991). Awaking the Heroes Within. New York: HarperCollins.

Panchadasi, S. (1915). The Astral World: Its Scenes, Dwellers and Phenomena. Chicago: Advanced Thought.

Perkins, J. (1990). Psycho Navigation. Rochester: Destiny.

Popescu, P. (1991). Amazon Beaming. New York: Viking.

Powell, A. E. (1927). The Astral Body. Wheaton: Theosophical.

Putnam, F. W. (1989). Diagnosis and Treatment of Multiple Personality Disorder. New York: The Guilford.

Radin, D. L. (1997). The Conscious Universe. San Francisco: Harper Edge

Randles, J. (1990). Mind Monsters: Invaders from Inner Space. Northamptonshire: Aquarian.

Redfield, J. (1994). The Celestine Prophecy. Los Angeles: Time Warner Audio Books.

Robert G. J. & Dunne, B. J. (1987). Margins of Reality. New York: Harcourt Brace Jovanovich.

Robinson J. M. (Eds.). (1988). The Nag Hammadi Library. San Francisco: Harper.

Seligman, J. & Katz, S. (1985, June 10). *Vampire Diagnosis: Real Sick.* Newsweek. p. 72.

Sparrow, L., Embleton, P., Fili, K., Peterson, M. & Sloan, D. (1984). How to Discover Your Past Lives. Virginia Beach: A.R.E., Edgar Cayce Foundation.

Spence, L. (1994). The Magic and Mysteries of Mexico. North Hollywood: Newcastle.

Stevenson, I. (1993). *Birthmarks and Birth Defects Corresponding to Wounds on Deceased Persons.* Journal of Scientific Exploration, 7, 4, 403-416.

Summers, M. (1996). The Vampire in Europe. New York: Gramercy.

Tannahill, R. (1975). Flesh and Blood. New York: Dorset.

The Holy Bible. King James Version. New York: Collins' Clear-Type.

Tondriau, J. & Villeneuve, R. (1968). Devils & Demons: A Dictionary of Demonology. New York: Pyramid Communications.

Treece, P. (1989). The Sanctified Body. Liguori: Triumph.

Walsch, N. D. (1996, Book 1). Conversations with God: An Uncommon Dialogue. New York: G. P. Putnam's Sons.

Wolman, B. B. (Eds.). (1977). Handbook of Parapsychology. New York: Van Nostrand.

Wilson, I. (1988). The Bleeding Mind. London: Weidenfeld and NicOlsen.

Wilson, Jackie. (1960). Night. Brenswicks Records.

Wolf, F. A. (1991). The Eagle's Quest. New York: A Touchstone.

Wolman, B. B. & Ullman, M. (Eds.). (1986). Handbook of States of Consciousness. New York: Van Nostrand Reinhold.

Woolger, R. J. (1988). Other Lives, Other Selves. New York: Bantam.

Wright, W. A. (Eds.). (1936). The Complete Works of William Shakespeare. New York: Garden City.

Made in the USA